THE
GENEROSITY OF
GOD

JOSHUA BROWN

The Generosity of God

© Joshua Brown

www.joshuabrown.org

www.dreamcolumbia.com

ISBN: 978-0-578-92588-2

For media or speaking engagement inquires, please email *hello@dreamcolumbia.com*

I dedicate this book to my amazing wife,
my daughter, my mom, my dad, my brothers, my sister,
and my Dream Church family.

CONTENTS

INTRO

Tradition is great when it is orthodox. Tradition is deadly when it is drenched in unorthodox notions that have used the Bible to prove wayward thinking is correct. What most in the West recognize as Christianity today is far from the covenantal marriage of Christ and the Church found in the New Testament. Christianity was never supposed to be a religion. It has become a religion in light of our unwillingness to think as the early Church did.

Philosophy (the study of how we think) has been at war with theology (the study of God) since we shifted the Church into that which upkeeps our regional religious traditions. We are scared of studying how we think because it threatens to unmask what we believe about God. [Rather than embracing original revelations on how we can view scripture, God, or us, we insist on constantly warping the Word of God to fit within the framework of thinking we have inherited]

Thus, as I discuss later in this book, we have made our thinking infallible and the Bible flexible. The Church is quickly becoming irrelevant because of this paradigm. We must wake up and realize that how we have viewed or thought about some ideas taught in scripture is slightly off and that by rediscovering the right way of thinking, we will rediscover the beauty of the scriptures we hold so esteemed.

Philosophy and theology must be joined together in union if we are going to see God's kingdom come in creation, as he promised. The goal of this book is not to teach you what to think about God or anything else. The goal of this book is to be a seed of a shift in how we think to the point that we let the Bible be the immovable Word of God and our thinking about the Bible be flexible and submissive to original intent.

You will not find the answers to all of life's questions in this book; you will, however, find the ammunition needed to ask and receive, seek and find, knock and have it opened for you. Questions do not equal doubt when philosophy and theology are jointly working together. Questions are the discovery of the one you have put all of your trust in: Yahweh. You can, and should, give God a total and complete "yes," while also asking questions about this kingdom we have inherited. I want to understand the love of God, for example. Not because understanding will lead to me believing, but because I believe and want to understand the one I believe in.

As you read this book, my prayer is that you will feel the frequency of original design reverberate throughout your identity. When I sat down to write, I felt the best way to address the topic at hand was to address it from the perspective that God is so in love with us that his primary delight is in what he gives us. He enjoys what we have to give him, but he is enthralled with what he gives us that we receive with joy.

With open hands, open hearts, and open minds, we dive into the generosity of God.

CHAPTER 1

LIKE A CHILD

I am amazed at what I have learned by reading books to my daughter. Having been a dad for four years, I have read hundreds of books to her about love, joy, dealing with your emotions, childlike faith, and dream-stricken wonder. It astonishes me how the authors of these simple books can pack such profound philosophical mysteries into so few words.

One of my favorites is titled *"On the Night You Were Born."* I do not know if Nancy Tillman is born again, but I do know she has grasped what it means to be made fearfully and wonderfully in a way that silences some of the greatest Christian minds in modern scholarship. At the end of her now-famous classic, she states:

For never before in story or rhyme (not even once

upon a time) has the world ever known a you, my friend, and it never will, not ever again... Heaven blew every trumpet and played every horn on the wonderful, marvelous night you were born.

A children's book has a way of drawing you back to simpler times. Times before the hustle and bustle, corporate prowess, broken water heater, and paying the mortgage. Times when all you had to do were two things: have fun, and trust that mom and dad (or whoever raised you) had everything under control. If you think about it, the base of your ability to have fun was on how much you trusted in being provided with every meal, a room, a bed, and any other need that presented itself.

In the "good ol' days," it was easy to love, easy to trust, and easy to see that everything would be okay. You perceived that you were worthy of love even if no one ever told you were loved. I call this the childness of life. It is the state of being where you are guided not by experience, for you have had none, but by what is alive in your DNA: the newly knit innate understanding that in the image of God you find your existence. Surrounded by utter mystery in a world you have only inhabited for a handful of days, you find yourself in an indescribable familiarity. It is as if you have been here before, but you have never been here before.

It is no wonder that Jesus said only those who were capable of having "childlike faith" would inherit the kingdom of God. Jesus knew that unless we got back to the place where mystery evokes trust rather than skepticism, we would never be able to approach what is only approachable by way of extreme mystery: The Presence of God.

We have lost our childness. Our worship traded watercolor on a blank canvas for a weekly pious chore, and our prayers laid down exploration of our imagination for the disciplined act required by religion. When did wonder go from staring in awe of a burnt orange sunset to meeting our budget for the fiscal year, or God go from Papa to an unapproachable, angry, distant, and uninterested deity? I suggest this shift took place over time through a blend of experience and religion. With every bully, disappointment, mess up, broken friendship, hellfire and brimstone sermon, and Sunday school lesson about Armageddon, we slowly took control of our lives, thus relinquishing the need to trust anyone, particularly God.

As a child, God was the Papa invested in our secret conversations about how stars stay in the sky without falling or how oceans never seem to flow past the beach.

As a teenager, God was tolerant of sex-crazed thoughts and untamed lust; he was always disappointed but, because of Jesus, was always forgiving. As an adult, God is a thought. A thought often drowned in the sea of emails, phone calls, texts, and social media. A thought entertained as an emergency last resort but forgotten when things are "good."

Do you see the trend? The older we get, the more distant, disappointed, and uninterested God becomes to us. We assume he cares less and less about us, our lives, our dreams, and our ambitions. There is one problem with all of this talk about God changing throughout our lives: He does not change.

Hebrews 13:8, "Jesus Christ is the same yesterday, today, and forever."

If God does not change, maybe we are the ones who change. Could it be that we did not project our feelings and ideas onto God as a child because we were inexperienced at life? I believe so. We took God for who he is. We did not expect him to fit in our box; we dared to see if we could fit in his. He was Papa, who was always waiting for a game of hide-and-go-seek. He cared when we cried, laughed when we laughed, and was so proud of even the tiniest baby step.

The older we get, the less valuable we see ourselves. When we see ourselves as invaluable, we start trying to earn value by what we do. Then, we make God (the one who judges value) a deity who longs for us to offer Him the works of our hands. We give unto God but never receive from God. Why would he want to give us anything? Isn't he always waiting to strike the moment we slide into immorality?

I want to illustrate something personal that will guide this entire book. I had a series of encounters with God where I began to, finally, let my works die and breathe deep in the reality of who I am. During these encounters, God used the following to describe how he sees me:

My daughter writes me letters all the time. Her letters are usually not legible and covered in smudges from a PB&J sandwich or stickers torn and replaced on the letter five times. On their own, these letters have no worth. However, these very letters are my most prized possessions. Their value is not in the letters at all. Their value is in the fact that my daughter made them. The identity of the one who made that which is worthless on its own, gives it the utmost value.

God does not need what we have to offer. Our best alone is worthless to the one whom all things were created through and find their being in. Therefore, his desires are not in what we give but in how convinced we are that we are his children. Furthermore, because he desires to convince us of our identity, his nature toward us is not a deity begging to receive but a dad longing to give.

That is the generosity of God. It is the characteristic of God's nature that is both most important and least talked about than any other piece of his nature.

Romans 5:8, "While we were still sinners, Christ died for us."

Our most significant act of worship has nothing to do with giving God anything other than open hands, open hearts, relentless trust, and an unwavering yes. We can let works-based religion die in the truth that our works can never achieve what our rest can. Salvation is received, not earned. You do not receive salvation and begin a lifestyle of earning. You have already earned everything because of the incarnation.

We receive salvation and then, through awakening to who we were before we ever took a breath, receive righteousness, holiness, intimacy, faith, peace, hope, love, joy, patience, kindness, goodness, gentleness, and self-control. We are not images; we are image-bearers. All we can do is reflect the image we were made in. We are incapable of producing an image on our own because all things are created solely through (and for) him. We work against divine will when we buy into the falsehood that our works, before or after salvation, affect our identity. Our works are only good because of our ability to reflect in them the image that we first received.

As you read this book, we are going to take a journey together to rediscover what it means to be a kid again; to have "childlike faith." In the end, my prayer is that you are more convinced of your son or daughter status than ever before, for that is the life of the believer. The kingdom of God is not entered into by reading enough, praying enough, and serving enough, but by the fact that your blood is his and your DNA says, "this is my child in whom I am well pleased."

CHAPTER 2

BORN AGAIN

If you ask anyone around Easter or Christmas what the purpose of Jesus' incarnation was, they would say, "to take away our sins." While the death of Jesus did take away our sins, Jesus came to do something much more significant than give us a new moral compass. Jesus undid Adam's fall.

Let me ask you a somewhat philosophical question: If a sinner stops sinning, are they still a sinner?

You either answered, "of course!" emphatically, "absolutely not" determinately, or did not answer the question because you thought I was trying to trick you into something you would have to repent for later. Either way, how we understand this question is essential.

Sin is the action of a sinner. It is what sinners do.

Accordingly, to be saved, you must be, in the words of Jesus, born again (or born from beginning). Being born again is not a change in actions; it is a change in identity. If a sinner stops sinning by action alone, they are just a good sinner. Sin, in the Greek, is the word *hamartia* which comes from the words *ha* (negative) and *meros* (portion or form). To be in sin is to be without your proper form or identity. That's why your identity is not about your actions, your identity is about your form, which was reconciled to God anew and permanently through the cross and resurrection.

To describe this another way, let us take the childlike approach. Squirrels eat nuts. It is what they do. Say you have a squirrel in your yard that no longer enjoyed the taste of nuts and instead wanted to eat grass exclusively. Does the fact that the squirrel no longer eats nuts change the identity of the squirrel? Of course not. The only way to change the squirrel's identity is to change its biological makeup to no longer be a squirrel.

Though sin is what sinners do, the way to become a new creation is not to simply remove the action of sin but to be born again, as in the beginning. That is, to have the entire order of your identity transformed into the image of Jesus. To be born of God, through Jesus, as a son or daughter of God.

You might ask, "Didn't humans lose their original identity because of an action?"

Absolutely. Here is where we see the beauty of Jesus on full display. The action of Adam's sin is what veiled us from who we were in God. If the action of disobedience, or sin, is what veiled us, it makes sense that the action of perfect obedience would unveil us once again. We as humans were misplaced from our original design because of the identity that we inherited from Adam's fall. We were doomed to live in the dark forever due to our inability to be perfectly obedient on our own.

Revelation 13:8, "From the foundation of the world, Jesus was slaughtered."

God's plan from the very beginning was Jesus. It was not his backup plan; it was his first and only plan.

Remember, God's nature, as laid out in chapter one, is that of a giver. Often, theologians argue things like sovereignty or free will related to salvation when I think we have missed the whole point. God's plan, from the beginning, was Jesus because even the absolute best we could come up with cannot even come close to what we have access to through the accomplishments of God himself, through Jesus, on our behalf.

God's plan was always to give us salvation, never receive it from us. His affections for you are such that before you were born, before the first sunrise, before the ground and sky formed, he had the gift of acceptance and righteousness planned for you that you would only have to be bold enough to receive without merit.

When someone gives us an unexpected gift, our response is, typically, something like: "I cannot take this" or "I did not do anything to deserve this." We feel bad for receiving a gift we did not earn. We have been so indoctrinated with a post-modern mindset that everything has to be earned that we do not know what to do when we get something we never worked to receive. I believe this is why Christianity in its earliest and purest form is so difficult for most to comprehend today, yet so simple that even the lowest vagabond can access it.

For most Christians today, being "Christian" is a matter of what you do. If you do the right things, you make it to heaven but if do the wrong things, you find yourself in the lake of fire. If you paint this on the actual gospel background, you get something that does not quite line up with what Jesus or any of the New Testament writers spoke and wrote on.

John the Baptizer and Jesus both preached the same core message, in the gospels: *Repent for the kingdom of Heaven is at hand.*

Repentance in Greek is the word *metánoia*, and it has two primary meanings. The first has to do with changing your direction or turning to go the other way. The concept is that you have been doing things one way, but you begin doing those things another, better way through repentance. The other meaning has to do with changing your mind or how you think. You replace your old thought process with an entirely new thought process. It is literally, "coming to your senses."

Repentance is not saying you are sorry; repentance recognizes that the way you got to the thing you are saying sorry for is the wrong way, and you need another way to produce a different result. Therefore, repentance is achieved through reidentification by faith in Jesus, not saying no to the wrong things. You cannot make an apple tree produce oranges, but you can cut down the apple tree and plant an orange tree seed to produce oranges.

Jesus came because God wanted to get all of his kids back; God had to redeem how his lost kids viewed him as Papa. Jesus was the meek and mild Messiah wrapped in tender mercy and kindness with a fierce love that we had never perceived before. He was not a warrior; he was a prince of peace. Jesus so loved us that he gave his own life for us.

One of the most significant statements in scripture is what Jesus said to Phillip in *John 14:9*, which I will also refer to in the chapter on Jesus later in this book. He said,

"Whoever has seen me has seen the Father."

Amazing. The Israelite views of God the Father had gone so astray that when he sent himself in the form of Jesus, they did not recognize him. I believe we do this today. God reveals himself in the person of Jesus to be kind and gentle yet full of zeal to raise you to your designed purpose, and we miss him because he does not look like the god religion told us he was.

French Enlightenment writer known as Voltaire once said, "In the beginning, God created man in his image, and man has been trying to repay the favor ever since."

We struggle with who God is because we see him through ourselves. We attribute our nature to God. We see him as fickle, distant, capricious, and angry because that is, in essence, what we are. Since we bear his image, he must look like us. The truth, however, is that we are to look at ourselves through Jesus and attribute, through the person of Jesus, God's nature to ourselves. God's not stooping down to our standard, but he is elevating us to his in Jesus. We now have been so covered with Jesus that when the world sees us, they see him, and if they see him when they see us, they see the Father.

The definition of insanity is doing the same thing over and over, expecting a different result. For centuries, the church has teetered back and forth on what it means to be saved. The arguments are: if we over-teach grace, people will see it as a license to sin. If we over-teach works, people will see it as legalistic. My problem with both is that we miss what salvation truly is. It is inherited reidentification, not behavioral modification.

The difference is staggering. Jesus did not come to teach people how to act like God's children; he came to convince people they are God's children.

When I was in middle school, I started playing basketball. I had big aspirations to become the next Michael Jordan. I used to practice in my driveway as if I were on an NBA court. The way I talked, the way I played, and the shots I made in that driveway were, in my mind, professional. In reality, I was a middle school kid who was average in real action and not even good enough to be in a high school varsity game a few years later.

(I am not shaming myself, by the way. Football was my primary sport).

My actions in that driveway and reality in a game were two drastically different scenes. No matter how much I acted like an NBA player, it would never make me an NBA player. Only being chosen by an NBA team in the draft would make me an NBA player, and by inheriting that position, my actions would naturally flow from who I, if this scenario were to play out, was.

At the risk of oversimplifying, this is personal and profound. We believe changing our actions will change who we are. I call this the mask. We live in a culture that is passionate about the image that we portray to people. That image does not have to be perfect, but it sure has to make others think the person behind the image is perfect. Everything is social media-driven, and all of our hopes and aspirations have grown from comparing our image to someone else's (more on this later).

The law of the Old Testament was greatly misunderstood by most. It was never a law of works.

Though it included works, it was a law of covenant between God and his people. Being God's people was supposed to dictate their works. Instead, they tried to make their works dictate whether or not they were God's people. Jesus then comes as that very Word of God in flesh to show us the nature of the one who had been fascinated with humanity from the beginning.

God is not looking for a spotless record of deeds; he is looking for your "yes." Your inclusion in the work of Jesus makes you perfect in God's eyes, not your no to sin. Astonishingly, your inclusion is likewise so powerful, once awakened to, that it will produce a no to every other inferior thing. You do not need to learn how to say no to temptation; you need to give Jesus such a yes that it produces a no to everything that is not Father, Son, and Spirit.

John 3:3, "Jesus replied, 'I tell you the truth unless you are born again [or born from origin], *you cannot see the Kingdom of God.'"*

CHAPTER 3

A RETURNING HEIR

❧ ◆❧◆ ❧

One of Jesus' most memorable parables (or stories) is found in *Luke 15* and is widely known as the story of *The Prodigal Son*. A stubborn son asked his father for his estate share immediately rather than when his father died. In Middle Eastern culture, this would have been a great offense. It was as if he was saying, "I wish you were dead already."

The father granted the request and gave his two sons their share of his inheritance. The Greek literally states, *"he gave them his life."* Having received from the father what he wanted, he packed up and moved off to see the world. He splurged on all life had to offer and soon found his inheritance gone.

Famine struck the land, and with nothing left to his name, he begged a farmer for a job and became a farmhand. He was willing to eat from the same slop as the pigs he was feeding in his starvation. Then, an epiphany: He asked himself, *"why eat slop when my father's servants eat three healthy meals a day and have all they need? I will go home and beg for my father to have enough mercy on me to make me a slave in his house."*

He cleaned up, wiped the dirt out of his hair, and pulled the wrinkles out of his shirt. As he walked down the road, he saw in the distance the last turn in the wood that would lead to his father's house. He wondered what his father would think. Could he ever love me again? Could he tolerate me enough to make me his slave? Of course, I could never be his son again, but maybe, just maybe, if I make a good speech and act sorry enough, he will put me in the cabin with his other servants. At least I would have something to eat as a slave.

The son practiced his speech and finally built up the courage to round that faithful corner. He was reluctantly nervous as he slowly walked; right foot, left foot, right foot, left foot. He started to see the smoke from the cooking fire, then the house's roof, then some servants working in the field. Then, he saw the front porch. He looked around and did not see his father anywhere.

Through the deafening doubt in his head, he heard

a winded old man screaming, "My son! My son!" As he looked toward the sound, he saw Papa running as fast as he could run with tears pouring down his face. Locking eyes, the son saw what he did not expect: forgiveness.

A tender embrace lasted for what seemed like decades when the son realized he still messed up. There is no way, in his mind, one moment of reunion could cover all that he had wasted. He thought fast and began reciting the speech he had prepared on his way home.

Luke 15:21-24 TPT

"21 'Father, I was wrong. I have sinned against you. I could never deserve to be called your son. Just let me be — '

The father interrupted and said, 'Son, you are home now!"

22 Turning to his servants, the father said, 'Quick, bring me the best robe, my very own robe, and I will place it on his shoulders. Bring the ring, the seal of sonship, and I will put it on his finger. And bring out the best shoes you can find my son. 23 Let's prepare a great feast and celebrate. 24 For this beloved son of mine was once dead, but now he's

alive again. Once he was lost, but now he is found!'
And everyone celebrated with overflowing joy."

There is one major detail missing in this *Prodigal Son* story: the father never calls the son prodigal. Go back and read the whole story in every translation and see if you can find the father calling the son prodigal in any of them. You cannot find it. It is not there. Why then have we, for centuries, called this son prodigal?

Religion has a habit of calling us by our mess, even after Jesus has dealt with it. How can we seize the gifts of God while stuck in the chains of our past? Mike Bickle, from International House of Prayer in Kansas City, says, "it is dangerous to keep a record of something God does not keep a record of." We continue to bring up our disqualifications to God when he only knows us as unequivocally qualified because of the resurrection. After all, *Psalm 103:12* says, *"He has removed our sin as far from us as the east is from the west."*

God is trying to work good out of our past mess, but we will not let him because we keep our past around like a pet that we feed, walk, and snuggle. The father only saw his son. The son's actions did not change his blood. The father did not see his son's sonship as something to be earned; he saw it as something so solidified that nothing had the power to revoke it. He was an heir by blood, not merit.

Jesus tells this parable right after talking about the shepherd who would leave the 99 sheep to go after the one and a woman who had ten coins, each of such value she went through extreme trouble to find the one that was misplaced. In the context of all Jesus was teaching on, when he gives the story of the returning heir (as he will henceforth be known as), we see Jesus giving us insight into our natural worth. By solidifying our natural worth, he strips the power of the past out of our story.

We write our past in lead; God writes our future in ink. Lead can be erased but ink is permanent.

Another interesting observation you could make when reading this story is when the son left home, all he was concerned with was what he got from his dad, not his relationship with his dad alone. Upon coming back, he sought not his dad's possessions (in fact, he assumed he would not get any other possessions) but his dad's proximity. The dad was okay wasting possessions on a son he knew would throw them away to help the son realize it was never the possessions but proximity that made up their relationship.

To refer to a point I will expound upon in a later chapter, allow yourself to redefine *good* in light of

Romans 8:28. The word that Paul uses for *good* is the Greek word *agathos*, which means intrinsically good, whether you can see it or not because it originates with and is empowered by God. Paul is not talking about a temporary virtue that we would call good in our minute view of eternity; Paul is talking about what is truly good, whether or not we ever see it because it comes from God, who also carries it on.

Paul's life and the life of most early church disciples and apostles got dramatically worse after salvation, naturally speaking. Paul was on top of the religious world, was well educated, and had an excellent reputation. He persecuted these "wacky Christians," which made him even more popular to the Jewish and Roman leaders. Then something extraordinary happened: he met Jesus on the road to Damascus (which sounded eerily like "de-mask-us," but I digress) and eventually became the leading voice in spreading the gospel across the globe.

When you look at his life from a material point of view, you would say it was awful. By the time of his beheading, the Church had expanded. However, many people who were formerly with him had been turned away by false teachers and defectors. In fact, in *2 Timothy 1:15*, Paul laments, *"Perhaps you have heard that Phygelus, and Hermogenes and all the believers of Asia have deserted me because of my imprisonment."* In today's standard, Paul had an average ministry. A "blip" on the radar of ministerial success.

However, that is not how we view Paul at all. Paul was, outside of Jesus Christ himself, the most influential person in the New Testament and possibly the scriptures as a whole. How is this? I believe it is because we are now almost two thousand years removed from Paul and can see how things worked out on the grand, eternal scale. When asking the question, "was Paul's life worked out for good?" today, it would be met by a resounding, "yes!"

That definition of good is what Paul is talking about in *Romans 8:28*. This kind of good is worked out only for those who prefer God because only those who trust God to the point of preferring God can see *agathos*. Realization of this may take hundreds or thousands of years, if not longer. It is the good of the whole that God is concerned with, not the good of the moment. To take it a step further, is anything good at the moment if it does not end in the good of the whole?

Time is a blessing for those who trust God and a curse for those who love control. For the child of trust, time is something you find joy in as you discover, with every second, the faithfulness of a giving God. For the mature adult of control, time is a stressor. Because you can never have absolute control, any control you think you have is a myth. Your control is uncontrollable. You have a hard time sleeping, being present in the moment, and frequently look back to the past or into the future.

Jesus tells us not to worry about tomorrow because we cannot control it. Why try to attain something unattainable? You cannot control anything, but you can reject his control. You cannot change what is coming your way in ten years on your own, but you can reject the path he has laid before you so that it seems as if you have made another way. You have not. You have sent yourself into an abyss of meaninglessness; of nothingness.

There is only one image in creation: His. Anything other than the image of God that calls itself an image is simply a costume. The only one capable of producing an image is God, and the only image we are capable of reflecting is God's. When we reject his image, we do not start bearing another image; we cease bearing an image at all.

The same thing happens to our lives. When we reject what God calls good for what we think is good, we are not choosing another path in the plethora of paths laid before us. We are rejecting the only path. Life can only be found on one way and through one gate, which is the small and narrow one. When Paul talks about all things working for the good of those who prefer God, in love, he is saying the path of true goodness unfolds before the person who, with every step they take, says in total trust, "I want what you want."

Don't you see? The story of the returning heir was not about the heir at all. It was about the faithfulness and trustworthiness of the father. A Papa who knew the son would realize that life could only be found in one place: the father's house. Proximity, not riches, gave the son life to the full.

You can be poor and happy. Likewise, you can be rich and miserable. However, you cannot be near the feet of Abba and be full of anything other than joy.

God as a giver means any path we try to trod that originates in us is phony. The only path worth taking is the one received from the lovestruck heart of our God. Perhaps the writing that puts this analogy ideally is one of my life poems by Robert Frost called "*The Road Not Taken*."

Two roads diverged in a yellow wood,

And sorry I could not travel both
And be one traveler, long I stood
And looked down one as far as I could
To where it bent in the undergrowth;

Then took the other, as just as fair,
And having perhaps the better claim,
Because it was grassy and wanted wear;
Though as for that the passing there
Had worn them really about the same,

And both that morning equally lay
In leaves no step had trodden black.
Oh, I kept the first for another day!
Yet knowing how way leads on to way,
I doubted if I should ever come back.

I shall be telling this with a sigh
Somewhere ages and ages hence:
Two roads diverged in a wood, and I —
I took the one less traveled by,
And that has made all the difference.

The "road less traveled," if you will, is Jesus who calls to us, saying in *John 14:6*, *"I am the way, the truth, and the life. No one can come to the Father except through me."*

It does not matter how far you have run or how

much you have squandered; Papa is waiting on the front porch to restore you to your rightful place of proximity with him. He is working all things for your good, but your job is to trust him, prefer his ways, and let him redefine good for you. God's goodness is so much greater than our best.

CHAPTER 4

GOD WITH US

The absolute pinnacle in the characteristic of God's generosity is Jesus. Jesus is what everything past, present, and future hinges upon. He is our vision for the Old Testament and New Testament alike. I do not know if it is possible to have too high a Christology because of this man's absolute significance. I feel wholly inadequate to write on the person of Jesus yet must if we are to discuss God's generosity.

We first get insight into God's intention to carry out a covenant with his people in *Genesis 15*, when he enters into a covenant with Abraham. To understand this, I will take a heavy Jewish historically-influenced view of the story and give you buried insight within the text. Here is what it reads:

1 After this, the word of the Lord came to Abram in a vision: "Do not be afraid, Abram. I am your shield, your very great reward."

2 But Abram said, "Sovereign Lord, what can you give me since I remain childless and the one who will inherit my estate is Eliezer of Damascus?" 3 And Abram said, "You have given me no children; so a servant in my household will be my heir."

4 Then the word of the Lord came to him: "This man will not be your heir, but a son who is your own flesh and blood will be your heir." 5 He took him outside and said, "Look up at the sky and count the stars — if indeed you can count them." Then he said to him, "So shall your offspring be."

6 Abram believed the Lord, and he credited it to him as righteousness.

7 He also said to him, "I am the Lord, who brought you out of Ur of the Chaldeans to give you this land to take possession of it."

8 But Abram said, "Sovereign Lord, how can I know that I will gain possession of it?"

9 So the Lord said to him, "Bring me a heifer, a goat and a ram, each three years old, along with a dove and a young pigeon."

10 Abram brought all these to him, cut them in two
and arranged the halves opposite each other; the
birds, however, he did not cut in half. 11 Then birds
of prey came down on the carcasses, but Abram
drove them away.

12 As the sun was setting, Abram fell into a deep
sleep, and a thick and dreadful darkness came over
him. 13 Then the Lord said to him, "Know for certain
that for four hundred years your descendants will
be strangers in a country not their own and that
they will be enslaved and mistreated there. 14 But
I will punish the nation they serve as slaves, and
afterward they will come out with great possessions.
15 You, however, will go to your ancestors in peace
and be buried at a good old age. 16 In the fourth
generation your descendants will come back here,
for the sin of the Amorites has not yet reached its
full measure."

17 When the sun had set and darkness had fallen, a
smoking firepot with a blazing torch appeared and
passed between the pieces. 18 On that day the Lord
made a covenant with Abram and said, "To your
descendants I give this land, from the Wadi of Egypt

to the great river, the Euphrates — 19 the land of
the Kenites, Kenizzites, Kadmonites, 20 Hittites,
Perizzites, Rephaites, 21 Amorites, Canaanites,
Girgashites and Jebusites."

Typically, people read this chapter and quickly move on to the following, saying, "Cool! God made a covenant with Abraham. What is next?" However, when you see what is happening historically in this chapter, you will see Jesus all over *Genesis 15*.

Remember what led up to *Genesis 15*. We see the stories of creation, the fall, the first murder, the world that had gone wrong, and God removing unrighteousness from the world with a flood. God then gives another righteous man (Noah) the command he first gave Adam and Eve (be fruitful and multiply). Next, the Tower of Babel and the scattering of languages and Abram's (later Abraham) introduction and story. The world in its youth, biblically speaking, has already endured significant changes and shifts. God is about to give Abram a picture of his plans for the future of creation and humanity.

First, note that in Hebrew, breaking up what someone is speaking is a Hebraic way of separating different conversations. We see this in *verse 2*. Abram makes one statement, but the following statement is separated by the words, *"And Abram said."* Therefore within verse 2, Hebraically speaking, we have two different conversations happening. That means God did not respond to his first. Have you ever felt God did not respond to your prayers or requests? It is not that he is fickle or distant, but that he is purposeful and joined to you in everything he does. Silence is always on purpose, for our good. More on this later in this chapter.

Back to *Genesis 15* and what is happening in this seemingly odd scene. Did you catch that when the Lord tells Abram to get a heifer, a goat, and a ram, each three years old, along with a dove and a young pigeon, he does not mention cutting the heifer, goat, and ram in half? He only says to get them. Nevertheless, Abram takes it upon himself to cut them in half. Why? Simply put, Abram knew what God was asking him to do: set up a covenant.

In the ancient Eastern world, this covenant was a betrothal covenant that you made when you engaged someone. It was called a "Blood Path." In short, you would spill the blood of the animals, and the blood would run down this path (typically a crack in the ground or something similar). Then the groom and the bride's father would take turns stomping in the blood, wearing white clothing, until the blood got on their clothing. It was a symbol for the groom saying, "If I do not uphold my end of the covenant with your daughter, you can do this in my blood (I put my life on it)." It was a symbol for the father-in-law saying, "If I do not present the daughter I promised you, you can do this in my blood (I put my life on it)."

Something shocking happens by the time we get to *verse 12*. Abram has fallen asleep. After preparing the covenantal ceremony, Jewish traditions state that Abram had realized that there was no possible way he could uphold his end of a covenant with Creator God. Because of this, he sits and thinks so long that, as *verse 11* says, birds of prey start coming down to eat the carcasses of these animals he has cut, and after pushing them away, he falls asleep. I want us to understand who Jesus is in light of what happens after Abram falls asleep.

As Abram is dreaming, he is given insight into Israel's Egyptian slavery and, ultimately, their journey back into the promised land to occupy Abram's promised inheritance. Then, in the darkness of the night, a smoking fire pot and a blazing torch pass over the blood path. Most people read through this part and skip to the next, unaware of the significance here. What is passing over this blood path? Smoke and fire. Smoke and fire represent the presence of God throughout the Old (and New) Testament. There are two, not one, presences represented here.

The Lord was telling Abram that he would not only uphold his own end of the covenant, but uphold Abram's end of the covenant as well. The blood would be on God to cover for Abram should he or his descendants inevitably mess their end of the covenant up. God entered into covenant with Abram and demonstrated his willingness to remain in that covenant by putting himself on the line for both parties. Now we can see a direct pointing to Jesus. In the flesh as a man, Jesus was God whose blood was spilled on behalf of humanity so that humanity would forever be free to enjoy the covenant God so desperately wanted.

Jesus is both our way into covenant and our sustainment in the covenant. God not only gave us access to himself through Jesus, but he also took on the role of keeping us in his hands through Jesus. Jesus lived as us so that by his spilled blood, we could live as him. Our blood could not satisfy covenant with God, for it was entered into with the requirement of God's blood, as seen in Jesus. Jesus did not just die the death we owed; he died the death required for our covenant. Did we deserve death? Yes. However, Jesus did not come to give us what we deserved based on our actions; Jesus came to give us what we deserved based on God's covenant. The death Jesus paid was much higher than simply freeing believers from hell. The death Jesus paid was to give humanity access to eternal covenant with the Trinity.

To celebrate that the cross canceled our sins alone stops grossly short of the extravagance of the cross and resurrection. The cross is a celebration of our access to the covenant which, of course, involves our sins being canceled but also involves many other things like being one with Christ, seated with Christ, and containing the Spirit of Christ. I do not want to make light of our removed sins because that is worth honoring; I simply want to elevate our honoring of all the other things the cross granted us to the level we have so honored our forgiven sins. I am not lowering either but raising both.

Jesus was different from the religious leaders of his time. He was more concerned with what people became than how people acted. The religious leaders ran from the sick; Jesus healed them. The religious leaders sided with the rich for personal gain; Jesus sided with the poor at the expense of personal gain. The religious leaders crafted scripture to fit the narrative they wanted to push into the culture. Jesus revealed scripture in the narrative God intended. The religious leaders wanted others to die for not following the law of Moses. Jesus was willing to die for those who did not follow the law in order to give them a new way "in."

Jesus makes a statement, which we briefly discussed in the chapter on being born again, in *John 14:9* to Phillip, who asks to see the Father, that shakes history to its very core:

"Anyone who has seen me has seen the Father."

In that moment of declaration, Jesus permits us to find everything we could know about the Father in him. Jesus Christ is perfect theology. What is my primary basis for believing in the generosity of God? Jesus. What is my primary basis in believing God is kind? Jesus. What is my primary basis for having hope? Jesus.

The Bible climaxes at this moment just before the passion story of the cross. God, having never forgotten his covenant, became flesh and dwelled in us. Emmanuel is the signpost that you and I are the object of God's affections. We are not talking about hype gospel, but true gospel. If you see Jesus and respond by thinking that grace is just your ticket to do whatever you want with no consequences, you have not seen Jesus. One look into the person of Jesus causes everything in my bones to shake. It causes me to shift everything in my life to submit to the one who walked the blood path on my account.

Our culture today does not know the true Jesus. They know a version of apathetic, complacent Jesus that turns the other way when people mess up and call it love and grace. They know a version of Jesus who is distant, separate, and floating around somewhere in outer space, too busy to want anything to do with them. Alternatively, they know a version of Jesus who is the Son on which God enjoyed unleashing his wrath. They do not want God because if he loved killing his son, he would love nothing more than to kill a less-than-perfect them too.

What we need is a revolution of sons and daughters who know the real Jesus. The one who is kind, patient, gentle, cutting, loving, healing, and the like who is not just close; he is one with us. God did not enjoy spending his wrath on his Son; his Son took his wrath on himself to finish Adam's death forever. God spent all of his judgments toward us on Jesus at the cross. There is no more judgment in Christ because our judgment took place on a cross two thousand years ago.

If Jesus died as us, he also was raised as us. His death gave us access to the covenant; his resurrection gave us access to his kingdom. Jesus gave us our image back. By inheriting our image again, we also get our garden. All of this, because of Jesus.

You could not write enough books to describe the magnitude of Jesus Christ and what he shows us about God's generosity, let alone a write a chapter. Nonetheless, I hope this serves as a marker to send you in a new direction of discovery for yourself. We are not awestruck by Jesus anymore because we do not know who he is. Sweet tea is good as long as there is not too much water added to it. You can so water it down that it does not taste good anymore, even if the substance of what was good is still floating around somewhere in the jar.

We have so watered down and legalized the gospel that we have not joined our minds to the authentic Jesus. He is our bridegroom. He is the one who calls us lovely. *John 17* shows that the Father loves us with the same love that he loves his Son with. Think of it: The measure of love he gives Jesus is the same measure of love he gives us. That is how much we are worth to him. Not only because he formed us from desire, but because he drenched us in the blood of the ever-fulfilled covenant between humanity and God.

> *Isaiah 59:21, "'As for me, this is my covenant with them,' says the Lord. 'My Spirit who is on you, will not depart from you, and my words that I have put in your mouth will always be on your lips, on the lips of your children and on the lips of their descendants – from this time on and forever,' says the Lord."*

Chapter 5

Lifestyle of Trust

━━━━━━━━━━ ◆◆◆ ◆ ━━━━━━━━━━

We love an underdog story. You know, the one where the scrawny athlete that no one thought would ever get a chance to play has their moment due to some unrealistic turn of events. They have the winning play and win the championship for the first time in their school's history and, of course, become legendary.

At some point in those stories, you will almost always see a coach or fan say something like, "I have faith in you." Telling you, "I have faith in you" translates, in English understanding, as me believing highly in your ability to perform a task. To be specific, faith is a complete trust or confidence in someone or something. While closely related to biblical faith, there is a critical difference that gets to the heart of God as a giver.

The New Testament idea of faith is not a conjured-up belief. There is no measuring stick of belief that says, "when you reach this amount of belief, you have faith." Religion has often taught followers that they are not seeing breakthroughs or answered prayers because they do not believe enough. Again, we run into our little foe: the works-based mindset, thinking that we can work our way, or in this case believe our way, into the things of God.

Faith, biblically speaking, is not how much you believe. Faith is the Greek word *pistis*. HELPS word studies defines it like this:

> *Faith (pistis) is always a gift from God and never something produced by people. In short, faith (pistis) for the believer is "God's divine persuasion" – and therefore distinct from human belief (confidence), yet involving it. The Lord continuously births faith in the yielded believer so they can know what he prefers, i.e., the persuasion of his will.*

> *In secular antiquity, pistis referred to a guarantee or warranty. In scripture, pistis is God's warranty, certifying that the revelation He in-birthed will come to pass (His way).*

Faith is the marrying of God's given revelation and our trust that his revelation will come to pass as he said, when he wants. Faith is a gift from God that we leverage by simply saying yes and trusting that he watches over his word to perform it (see *Jeremiah 1:12*).

A famous passage that every believer has heard quoted countless times to argue for an English perspective of faith is the passage found in *Matthew 17*. Jesus had just experienced the most significant encounter in history with God: the transfiguration. When he comes down from that encounter, the disciples who were not with him on the mountain were trying to cast a demon out of a boy with no success. Jesus casts it out for them and says this to them when they ask why they could not cast it out on their own:

> *Matthew 17:20, "He replied, 'Because you have so little faith. Truly I tell you, if you have faith as small as a mustard seed, you can say to this mountain, 'Move from here to there,' and it will move. Nothing will be impossible for you.'"*

It was *"because of your little faith."* There is so much depth we miss in the English bible because our language is simple. It is one of the simplest languages on earth. In one sense, having a simple language is why so many can learn it very quickly. In a biblical sense, we sometimes see words translated broadly because we lack the multiplicity of words seen in Greek.

Faith, here, is not *pistis*, as in every other "faith" translation in the rest of the New Testament, but the Greek word *oligopistia* that is only found one time in the bible: Here, in *Matthew 17:20*. It means "little faith." Now, think of what Jesus teaches. He said they could not cast the demon out because of their little faith (*oligopistia*), then said if they had faith (*pistis*) as small as a tiny mustard seed, they could do anything. Would not you call a tiny mustard seed little? It is, by definition, small. Elsewhere in the New Testament, the mustard seed is called the smallest of all seeds.

I've heard it said that revelation is in the tension that exists between two seemingly contradictory ideas. Jesus rebuked their little faith yet says they could have cast the demon out if they had little faith. When you see things like this in scripture, you should pause, reflect, dive deep, and discover where the living, breathing Word of God is calling you.

Remember, faith comes from God, and trust activates it. Jesus says if they have faith within them, even if it is as small as a mustard seed, they have the potential to do anything. So, was Jesus rebuking them because they lacked a God-given revelation of the boy's healing? That cannot be the case because when Jesus encountered him, Jesus cast the demon out. Therefore, we can mark off the component of faith that comes from God as being in question. When we do this, trust, in what God had inbirthed, is left in question.

The Complete Jewish Bible translates this verse, *"Because you have such little trust! Yes! I tell you that if you have trust as tiny as a mustard seed, you will be able to say to this mountain, 'Move from here to there!' and it will move; indeed, nothing will be impossible for you!"*

The lifestyle of trust says, "I give you control, you hold my world and my destiny in your hands, and I will move by your word alone." God being a giver is God giving what is good. Sometimes, this means God first taking away. The allusion many live in is that because they are complete, life is good. The believer's goal is not to just be full, but to be full of the right thing: Jesus.

If you have a good life, a good job, a good spouse, and go to church, you are full. However, that does not define Christianity. That is secularism with a label. Christianity says if I am empty of secularity but filled with Jesus, I am full, and God is good. Only the one who has committed themselves to trust can be aware that they are full of Jesus.

We have a habit of fighting against God. In the Enlightenment Period, much of the Western world shoved God into the distance to run the world as they wanted. They separated intimacy with God from the works of a believer. In the wake of this, we have generations that think that as long as they check off the right boxes, they are good Christian men or women. As stated in previous chapters, thinking like this defines religion. True Christianity, however, requires the trust that comes from an intimate, covenantal relationship with another, particularly God, through Jesus.

In his book *The Great Divorce*, C.S. Lewis states, "There is but one good; that is God. Everything else is good when it looks to Him and bad when it turns from Him." My leaning in teaching is what I call Philosophical Theology. I like to challenge how I and others think, mainly related to God and his kingdom.

If I were to ask you what is good, you would give me a list of things you enjoy or desire (without this book's context)—those *things* are products, not originators. I agree with the law that everything comes from something. Nothing comes into being without coming from something else. One of the greatest proofs for God's existence is that Christianity offers the best explanation for the origination of all things: God. You cannot have a flower without a flower seed.

Without spending too much time explaining deep philosophical reasoning, good is, at its core, that which produces all good things. For example, a car can be a good thing or a bad thing. The car does not change, but the driver does. A car is good for the clear-minded adult who has both hands on the wheel and is aware of their surroundings. A car is terrible for the drunk who cannot walk straight. Therefore, a car is defined as good or bad depending on its driver.

All things in our lives we call good are horrible if they did not come from the only one who is good, God. At the same time, all things in our lives we call bad are excellent if they came from God. We inherit a new lens to see everything in our world through when we transition from a life of skeptical religion to trusting intimacy. If God is good and if he, therefore, works all things together for my good, I, as a believer in covenant with God, have one possible outcome in life: good.

Trust is something that you grow in overtime. When my wife and I first met, I had walls built up that did not come down overnight. Nevertheless, over a year, every minute we spent together, I saw more and more that I could trust her with my life. After six years of marriage, I can say that she has done everything for my good, in every season of our relationship. Even every argument and disagreement was rooted in the truth that she wanted what was best for me and our relationship.

When you start to see things in light of trust, you feel weight, pressure and, yes, anxiety begin to fall off of your shoulders in chunks. All of our issues in intimacy with God come from an inability to state wholeheartedly, *"the Lord gives, and the Lord takes away; blessed be the name of the Lord."* God is nothing but good, which means he can give nothing but good, even if we see it, in moments, as bad in our frail human thinking.

Romans 8:28, as mentioned in the chapter on the Returning Heir, has some interesting Greek wording. Earlier I summarized the difference between Greek and English, which is just as relevant when it comes to this verse. In English, we have one word for love: love. In Greek, there are many words for love, each describing a specific kind of love.

> *Romans 8:38, "And we know that in all things God works for the good of those who love him, who have been called according to his purpose."*

While waiting on a midweek service at our church recently, I felt led to do a quick study on what it means, in this verse, to "love God." It struck me when I saw that the word Paul uses here is not *phileo* (friendship love) but *agapaó* (the most intimate love used for a bride and groom). *Agape* means to prefer. The evincing of your love for God is whether you prefer what he prefers or what you prefer. Is my wife my friend? Absolutely. However, she is my bride. She is not a casual relationship; she is my most intimate relationship.

Is Jesus our friend? Sure. However, if we stop there, we have stopped crucially short. *All things work together for the good of those who*, let us say, *prefer God*. That changes how we see this verse and others. Trust says, "I prefer you, Abba." Trust transitions from what I want to what he wants. He is not our copilot; he is the only pilot.

"All men's miseries derive from not being able to sit in a quiet room alone." - Blaise Pascal.

Is it possible that our culture's redemption will not come through us doing the right things but us hearing the right things? *Romans 10:17* reminds us that *"faith comes from hearing..."* When we begin to trust what we hear, we will begin to do what creation is standing on tip-toe waiting for: not good ministry, but sons and daughters manifesting the image of their Creator.

The major step in leveraging what God gives is trusting God is good.

Chapter 6

The Secret Place

I got my driver's license in 2007. I will never forget the feeling I had when I got behind the wheel of a car for the first time alone. It seemed as if all possibilities were ahead of me. Hearing the engine roar on, backing out onto the asphalt road, putting the car in drive, and accelerating forward were some of the most infamous moments of my life. I wanted to drive everywhere. It was new, exciting, and gave me my first real sense of independence.

Now, I have been driving for over a decade. Getting in a car and driving somewhere seems more like a chore than an adventure. What was once something I enjoyed is now just a means of getting from one place to another. I have become apathetic toward driving. My apathy has grown not because I have had very little access to a car over the past decade, but because

I have had an abundance of access to a car. The more I drive, the more it becomes routine.

In life, we lose awe for something the more we encounter it. Having food to eat, for example, is normal for us. However, in Africa's bush, having food to eat on a particular day is a cause for celebration because it is rare. We should celebrate how much access we have to what others consider rare rather than allowing that access to grow us cold.

Cold, unfortunately, is how most grow toward God. As God gives us more access, it often results in access becoming normal. For highly persecuted Christians in China, it is unfathomable to have unlimited access to a church and other believers out in the open. We, in the West, will skip out on church if the weather is not perfect. This passivity is what I refer to as apathy. In terms of zeal, the greatest believers usually have lived a season or a life of restriction.

The issue is how we determine value. In economics, rarity equals value. We are seeing this play out right now with cryptocurrency, such as bitcoin. Its value has been at record highs because only a certain amount of bitcoins exist, and more are being discovered and owned each week. The fewer bitcoins there are available, the rarer they become; thus, their value increases. If you were to triple the number of bitcoins that existed, the value would plummet because it would become less rare.

I am not writing a book on economics or bitcoin, but I am trying to recognize how we determine value based on rarity. The same is valid throughout the Old Testament as well. Only specific individuals could access the Presence of God at certain times. No one else, no other time. We honor what we value. If we value what is rare, we will honor what is rare. If we grow apathetic toward accessibility, we will not honor accessibility.

A more pertinent example of this would be marriage. We know all too well the older couple married for 50 years that barely coexist in the same house, let alone love each other. If you could travel back in time to their wedding day, I bet you would not find a couple angry and lonely but giddy and intimate. Time and access have caused them to grow complacent rather than more giddy and more intimate. They no longer honor their covenant because they have lost value in it. It has become robotic and religious.

The kingdom does not work like the culture around us does, and the only way for us to see that is to rewire our determination of value. In the kingdom, value is not determined by rarity but by abundance. The more you have, the higher the value. To use the example from the Old Testament, God's once rarely accessed Presence is now not only readily available to all but living within our very person all the time. We do not have to go to a location to encounter the Presence of God; we are the Presence of God. We are the location where others encounter the Presence of God. That abundance has caused Presence not to lose value but to gain immense value.

The Israelites never saw this. God wanted to give them all of himself, but the more he gave them, the more they seemed to take it for granted. He continually had to remind them of the poverty and brokenness of what life is like apart from him to get them back to the place of value and honor for what they exclusively accessed. What if we were the start of a legacy that did not make the same mistake? What if glory to glory meant higher value to higher value and higher honor to higher honor?

Deep intimacy with our bridegroom king, Jesus, is in our core. We were made to be always satisfied but never satisfied. That is, we are always satisfied with the measure of Presence God has given us, but we refuse to stop at this level. The question is not how much God wants to give us, for he, being generous, always wants to give us everything he has. The question is how much we are willing to receive. How much we are willing to receive is greatly determined by how we value and honor what we already have. God loves us too much to give us more of what has, up to this point, caused us to grow apathetic. It would be *good* for him to remove what we have grown complacent toward, for a season, to reinvigorate our hunger and value toward it.

Since being born again, no other set of scriptures have come close to impacting me like the book of *Song of Songs*. Growing up, we skipped this book because it was the sex book, and we did not want to do anything to cause a bunch of already sex-crazed teenagers to think about sex even more. However, looking back, *Song of Songs* was no doubt what would have saved me many years of thinking God was ready to reject me at any moment.

Song of Songs has been a perplexing book for centuries. There was great debate about whether or not to include it in the canon of scripture. *Song of Songs* is titled using the same linguistic technique as *Holy of Holies*. More precisely, *Song of Songs* is the song of all songs, as the *Holy of Holies* is the holy of all holies. There have been more interpretations of *Song of Songs* than any other book in scripture. The early interpretation, and the one that I hold to, is allegoric. By seeing the text allegorically, the man symbolizes God, and the woman symbolizes Israel. On the other side of the cross of Jesus, we can say the man symbolizes God expressed in Jesus, and the woman represents the Church expressed in you and I.

When you read *Song of Songs* with the eyes of this being a love letter between us, the bride, and Jesus, our bridegroom king, you find yourself immersed in identity, intimacy, and covenant. In short, *Song of Songs* describes an access we never knew we had. The book starts with the key to unlocking the rest of the depth within these eight short chapters.

Song of Songs 1:2-4a TPT

2 Let him kiss me with the kisses of his mouth – for your love is more delightful than wine.

3 Pleasing is the fragrance of your perfumes; your name is like perfume poured out. No wonder the young women love you!

4 Take me away with you – let us hurry! Let the king bring me into his chambers.

Count how many times you see the word *let* or

take. If you counted four total, you were correct. In four verses, she gives four separate commands of permission to him before he ever says a word. *Let him kiss me, take me away with you, let us hurry, let the king bring me into his chambers.* All of these are saying, "I give you permission to …"

The first step to intimacy with Jesus is permission. We must give Jesus permission to undo what needs to be undone and draw us to places we did not think we would ever go. Permission denotes honor and trust. At the core of the matter, permission is given to what you value as worthy of having it.

The Shulamite woman, who symbolizes us, is saying, "I value my beloved to the point that I give him permission to shift my world." We struggle with permitting Jesus. Sometimes, we struggle because the Church or someone in ministry has let us down; other times, we have unresolved doubt. Nevertheless, permission is the key that unlocks the door to intimacy. If we are going to get to the place of value, trust, and honor, that permission requires, we will have to deal with what has kept us from being in that place.

Doubts about God and how he operates can keep you from trust in God. We are only willing to permit someone we totally and ultimately trust. The solution to the problem of doubt is a realization that in the West, particularly in the American South, we do not believe God's Word is infallible (meaning incapable of making mistakes or being wrong). We believe our way of thinking is infallible and make the Word of God fit within our way of thinking. When we say the Word of God is *infallible* what we are honestly saying is, "how we view the Word of God is infallible." I happen to believe no English bible can be truly infallible because of the language barrier between the original text and the simplicity of English. That does not make it any less important; it simply requires us to lean on the original Hebrew and Greek for true infallibility.

Most doubt comes from an unwillingness to have your thinking tinkered with and a total willingness, though subconsciously, to have the scriptures shifted into what they were never supposed to be. I am faced with one example frequently in leading many young adults when they ask how a good God could send people to hell. They question passages of the Bible that seem to be, on the surface, describing an angry God having a good time demolishing people groups. We should be questioning our understanding of both the Bible and the nature of God, not the other way around. We default to "how could God…" when we should default to, "why do I see this passage as…" We carry this pride, since the Enlightenment Period in the West, that we know everything and have an understanding of how things ought to be. Apart from God, we have neither.

You can and should have questions and trust at the same time. I will not question the absolute perfect and without flaw nature of our Creator God, but I am great with continually questioning how I see the absolute perfect and without flaw nature of our Creator God. It is my thinking and perspective, not God's nature, that needs to be redeemed.

Now, back to *Song of Songs*. When you read through the book in its entirety, you see that the Shulamite woman goes back and forth between giving her king permission, and letting her doubts retract that permission. There is even a moment where she decides she cannot make the journey with him because of *the shadows,* or the unknowns, where trust is required.

Song of Songs 2:17 TPT

17 Until the day breaks and the shadows flee, turn, my beloved, and be like a gazelle or like a young stag on the rugged hills.

What precedes this response is a dare by the

bridegroom to *arise and come with him (Song of Songs 2:13 TPT)*. We know what this back and forth is like because that has been most of our stories. There are days we permit him to operate however he wants, then retreat to what is comfortable the next day. Eventually, we grow weary with the seesaw of emotions and slide into a life of comfortability, where there is no permission required and no unknowns. Religion is doing what looks like all the right things but never actually doing the only right thing.

Doubt hides behind a veil called being smart. You know, those who say, "be smart with your decisions" are saying, "do not do anything out of the ordinary." By out of the ordinary, we mean out of the comfortable. Most Christians live with doubt and have no relationship with Jesus. They are born again by label, not by identity. They do not permit because permission means trust, and trust means, for a season, uncomfortability.

The great news is there is a solution to the seesawing. It is called the secret place. The secret place is the place of intimacy between you and your king, Jesus, where you can lay your doubt, questions, and uncertainty at his feet and let him tell you why you can give him permission. The place where he shows you what you were made for and gives you a blueprint that seldom fits within the mold of traditional culture. The place where you learn his proximity alone is worth laying down your life.

I spent my whole life, up to age 24, going through the motions and having to convince myself that trusting God was what I should do. I would hold on to biblical promises like they were my raft in the middle of the ocean, keeping me afloat. I had doubts about his goodness because, in all honesty, I did not know him. I knew about him, but I did not know him. It is hard to put your life in the hands of someone you know about from a book but have never had a relationship with in real life. That all changed when, in 2015, the Lord radically shifted my world. It started with me finally giving him full permission to, in the words of *Song of Songs*, "*bring me into his chambers*." I started making his presence and the secret place the purpose of my life.

Not surprisingly, I found myself living with what those around me called a supernatural faith in God. I do not know if it was supernatural or my natural identity being brought back into its correct function. Either way, things that used to be impossible became default because I fell in love with the man named Jesus rather than the religion of ideas and thoughts about the man named Jesus. I finally believed I was the righteousness of God in Christ Jesus because Jesus reminded me of that every day. I lived convinced that God is good, not because a circumstance played out in my favor, but because I saw the eyes and heard the voice of the one whose frequency has one sound: goodness. My circumstances, in general, became irrelevant because I knew Jesus and knew that he genuinely had my world in his hands.

I did not have all of my questions answered, but I inherited a new way of thinking which has opened me up to see the answers that were always in front of me. I did not need to look at new scenery; I needed the correct prescription in my lenses to see the same scenery correctly. Your life calling is ultimately the place where you and Jesus commune every day. To this day, I get up early in the morning, before the sun comes up, and spend hours with my beloved. I do not know how to do anything else. Once you get a taste of closeness, you will never have to convince yourself to give him permission in your world again. You will have an open-ended yes because you know he can be nothing but faithful to those who prefer him.

Having said all of this about the secret place, we can finally see how the kingdom man or woman determines value. Not by rarity anymore, but by abundance. More specifically, abundance as in proximity. Abundant access to nearness with Jesus draws you to the place where, even when the shadows are the direction he calls you to, you give him unlimited permission. You permit who you honor and trust, and you give honor and trust to whom you know most intimately.

When the secret place is the tree of your life, the fruit will come effortlessly. Give him a yes to a relationship, which will always result in a yes to everything else. Know him, be known by him, and build him a place to rest consistently, with you, every day. That is the secret place.

CHAPTER 7

THE POISON OF COMPARISON

—◆ ►◆◄ ◆—

In his book "Ruthless Trust," Brennan Manning tells a story that I think illustrates comparison in a way all can relate to. He writes:

> *A water-bearer in India had two large pots. Each hung on opposite ends of a pole that he carried across his neck. One of the pots had a crack in it, while the other was perfect. The latter always delivered a full portion of water at the end of the long walk from the stream to the master's house. The cracked pot arrived only half-full. Every day for a full two years, the water-bearer delivered only one and a half pots of water.*

> *The perfect pot was proud of its accomplishments,*

because it fulfilled magnificently the purpose for which it had been made. But the poor cracked pot was ashamed of its imperfection, miserable that it was able to accomplish only half of what it had been made to do.

After the second year of what it perceived to be a bitter failure, the unhappy pot spoke to the water-bearer one day by the stream.

"I am ashamed of myself, and I want to apologize to you," the pot said

"Why?" asked the bearer: "What are you ashamed of?"

"I have only been able, for these past two years, to deliver only half my load because this crack in my side causes water to leak out all the way back to your master's house. Because of my flaws, you have to do all this work and you don't get full value from your efforts," the pot said.

The water-bearer felt sorry for the old cracked pot, and in his compassion, he said, "As we return to the master's house, I want you to notice the beautiful flowers along the path." Indeed, as they went up the hill, the cracked pot took notice of the beautiful

*wildflowers on the side of the path, bright in the
sun's glow, and the sight cheered it up a bit.*

*But at the end of the trail, it still felt bad that it had
leaked out half its load, and so again it apologized to
the bearer for its failure.*

*The bearer said to the pot, "Did you notice that
there were flowers only on your side of the path,
not on the other pot's side? That is because I have
always known about your flaw, and I have taken
advantage of it. I planted flower seeds on your side
of the path, and every day, as we have walked back
from the stream, you have watered them. For two
years, I have been able to pick these beautiful flowers
to decorate my master's table. Without you being
just the way you are, he would not have had this
beauty to grace his house."*

The cracked pot saw itself as a failure; the water-
bearer saw the cracked pot as perfect, exactly how it
was. How is it possible to have two vastly different
views of the same thing? The cracked pot didn't see
how beautifully the bearer was leveraging its cracks to
bring forth what no perfect pot ever could; all it saw
was the other pot doing what it could not. The water-
bearer knows the pots' differences and celebrates those

as unique and vital parts of the master's house. One provides a full measure of water; the other provides a half-measure of water with a bouquet.

They both provide different things and are both needed by the master. If one starts trying to do what the other does, it will fail because it is designed differently. Not only that but in the process of mimicking another, the master (as it were) would miss out on what only the pot in its purest state can bring to the preverbal table.

1 Corinthians 12:27 TPT, "You are the body of the Anointed One, and each of you is a unique and vital part of it."

God designed you very specifically. You are a fingerprint on creation, not a general stroke of thousands of humans. You are a unique, one-of-a-kind, crucial part of God's creative plan, and there is no one like you. God placed you in his creation as a word that delivers to the rest of his people, past, present, and future, a view of his image expressed solely in you.

Identity, like all other qualities in the kingdom, is a gift. Your uniqueness is not something you have to work at; it is something you naturally are. Your quirks, attitudes, personality, gifts, abilities, and more, are all received blessings from the heart of Abba. Who you are in your original state, untouched by the cliché hands of society and religion, is whom God wants you to be.

Nevertheless, we live in a world of comparison. Everyone wants to be anyone but themselves. We manufacture masks and spend our days making sure they are clean, polished, and on display. We show people what we think they want to see and hide what we think they do not want to see: our true selves. All the while, who we authentically are gets buried deeper and deeper behind the lie that we are our mask.

Moms beat themselves up because they are not doing what other moms are posting on their social media page. Pastors leave the ministry because they could never get their church above 45 people, and the new church down the street with lasers launched with 450. Young adults feel guilty for not settling for their old relationships because everyone else around them is getting married and having kids. Christians avoid the secret place with Jesus because they are not hearing what their friends in the church are.

I could go on, but do you see how easily we reject our purpose because it is not like someone else's purpose?

The emotionally beat-up mom does not have her

child potty-trained by age 2 like some others, but she is present and a great listener when her child has something to say. The exiled pastor does not have hundreds of people and lasers, but he does have a group of people that have become family and are growing in their knowledge of Jesus in a way that the megachurch pastor wishes he had. The single young adult does not have a spouse, but they are learning what it means to be the bride of Christ and getting their life in such an order that when the right one does come along, they will be able to dive headlong into love's excellent adventure. The downcast Christian may not be hearing tweet-able phrases in the secret place, but they are hearing the whispers that are building their internal world on the rock of our salvation, and as I recall, Jesus said the last are first in his kingdom.

You could be right in the middle of the path God laid for you yet perceive yourself as a failure because you aren't living up to someone else's standard. Nothing blinds us more to God's generosity than having our eyes on someone else. It is a poison that kills purpose quickly and sometimes permanently.

Comparison is so dangerous because it disguises itself as inspiration. Though inspiration is exemplary in its rawest form, typically we want to be who inspires us. The moment we start wanting to be like someone else, we cease being ourselves. The only identity we can become is our own. We fail 100% of the time at being someone else. The only inspiration worth indulging in should push you deeper into Jesus and self.

I have given many sermons over the past four years, hundreds to be exact. It never fails that the ones I think will be world-changing end up being average, and the ones I think will flop, world-changing. I like to think God is comical by humbling my best and exalting my average. I used to be frustrated by his wit until I stopped to think about how I define "best" and "worst." Best, for me, was how much my sermon sounded like a big-time pastor's sermon and worst was how much my sermon sounded like, well, me.

Over time, I had to learn how to be happy with what Joshua produced from the authentic Joshua, being led by the Holy Spirit, of course, and reject what I created from a false Joshua that was a cover sermon of someone else. I know most people reading this book are not pastors, so that particular scenario may not relate. However, altering who we are to fit a standard we have adopted through comparison is all too familiar. We need you as you, and you need me as me.

Look at another part of the *1 Corinthians 12 TPT*

passage I mentioned earlier in this chapter:

> *14 ... the human body is not one single part but rather many parts mingled into one. 15 So if the foot were to say, "Since I'm not a hand, I'm not a part of the body," it's forgetting that it is still a vital part of the body. 16 And if the ear were to say, "Since I'm not an eye, I'm not really a part of the body," it's forgetting that it is still an important part of the body.*

> *17 Think of it this way. If the whole body were just an eyeball, how could it hear sounds? And if the whole body were just an ear, how could it smell different fragrances? 18 But God has carefully designed each member and placed it in the body to function as he desires. 19 A diversity is required, for if the body consisted of one single part, there wouldn't be a body at all! 20 So now we see that there are many differing parts and functions, but one body.*

Living in comparison is not only robbing your identity, it is robbing God of glory. The root of worship is authenticity. We trample on the gift of God-given us when we bring God our mask that looks like whom we think he wants to see. He does not want the you that hides all your cracks in shame; he wants the you who exposes all your cracks, proud of what he has been able to accomplish with them.

Comparison is a topic that deserves many books. It is multifaceted and can change legacies. However, it does have its place in understanding how we steward the gift of identity (we will talk stewardship later in the book). The world around us wants us to fit the mold it has created. Religion wants us to live the life it has demanded. Jesus wants us to stop trying to be something we are not and simply receive the image we were born to carry, innately.

Saint Augustine of Hippo said, "God loves each of us as if there were only one of us."

I do not know if you ever heard this in the church you grew up in, but I heard the following on a near-weekly basis: "Jesus would have still died on the cross if you were the only one on earth." At my worst, I questioned that phrase. Was I worth it? Was anyone worth it? Alone, of course not. We cannot achieve worth on our own; it does not originate in us. Worth originates in God. It is inherited, not gained.

Therefore, worth is not the measure of what you have done but how much you are you. Once this starts to take root in our minds and our spirits, we can finally feel the weight of comparison fall away. We do not have to be what everyone else is. We do not want to be what everyone else is. The kingdom is advanced when a thumb stops trying to be a foot and becomes resolute in its willingness to become a great thumb.

That is, after all, the only thing it is truly capable of being.

Chapter 8

Dream Again

—◆—

Human beings are natural dreamers. We do not grow out of our imaginations in adulthood, we learn to say no to our imaginations in light of feeling secure. The villain that torments the dreamer within is security, also known as living "safe." In finances, people like investing in low-risk stocks to make a good return on their money without the risk of losing everything if the stock market turns negative.

You know the drill: a great idea pops in your head that looks like everything you have dreamed of your whole life. Then you remind yourself that by pursuing that, you would be risking everything you have built. After that, you remind yourself about the fail-rate for those who pursue their dream. Finally, you end up feeling a sense of safety in living average, and you shove your dream down further and further until you eventually forget you ever had a dream.

Fixing our view of God to be who he truly is (a giver), allows us to regain one of the most God-like qualities of our image-bearing capacity: The ability to dream. *Ephesians 3:20* says that *God can do immeasurably more than all we could ask or imagine*. We are great at asking but well below-average at imagining. Asking can be passive. Asking can be a casual religious duty performed to say you did it. Imagining, however, takes genuine authenticity. The word imagination comes from the Latin word *imago* which means image. The future of our nations is dependent on the image you and I establish in them.

The real question is, what are your dreams? I do not desire to give you your dreams, but I do desire to get you to think higher about your dreams. First, let us look at what a dream is. Dream, in our sense, means a strongly desired goal or purpose. It is also something that fully satisfies a wish. The more widely used definition for a dream is, of course, a series of thoughts, images, or emotions occurring during sleep.

The New Testament and Old Testament alike are full of dreamers and their dreams. It is the primary way to Lord spoke to someone, mainly to give them a prophetic message. Why is this?

Job 33:15-18, "In a dream, in a vision of the night, when deep sleep falls on people as they slumber in their beds, he may speak in their ears and terrify them with warnings, to turn them from wrongdoing and keep them from pride, to preserve them from the pit, their lives from perishing by the sword."

God speaks through dreams because we have finally shut off our own opinions and distractions to hear him clearly. While asleep, he can give us what he thinks without our preconceived safety stepping in to interrupt anything too risky. The Hebrew word used here for a dream can be translated as "dreamer." It carries a connotation that the one who has these dreams from God has become a dreamer or can interpret a dream correctly. The Greek word for dream is very similar.

What is it about dreaming that causes hope to swell up in us about our authentic destiny and crippling fear of failure at the same time? Dreams are God's way of laying things out, often symbolically and creatively, in a way that reveals our future or details meanings in our past. Dreams are images we see when we sleep and strongly desired goals or purposes when we are awake. These are connected by idea, not just word.

The Lord plants prophetic seeds of his insight into

our being while we are at rest in ways we would never hear while awake. Seldom do we even remember what we dreamed. However, we are constantly dreaming, and many of those dreams are from the Lord.

The book of *Revelation* is a big dream that unveils the deeper meaning behind the events of scripture and the new creation. In *Genesis*, Jacob falls asleep and sees a latter with angels ascending and descending as a prophetic image of Jesus. Daniel becomes a powerful man in captivity because the Lord gives him insight into interpreting the dream of Nebuchadnezzar. I could go on, but the point is, God has given us countless material in scripture to make the conclusion that one of God's standard ways of speaking, for a good reason, is dreams.

When you dream of doing something or being something, you simply agree with the seeds of dreams the Lord planted in you while at rest. You may never realize this, but it has proven accurate time and time again. Jesus fulfilled countless dreams and visions through the incarnation. Prophets dreamed of God's kingdom reigning in the earth. Jesus came with the announcement that the kingdom was here. *Hebrews 11* goes through a list of those who saw things *"from a distance"* but never received them because they were looking for a heavenly country. This verse means they had visions and dreams of what was to come, primarily in Jesus, but never saw them in reality, and they were okay with that. They knew that when what they saw came to pass in reality, they, with us, would enjoy the fullness of what their fulfilled dream effectuated.

Even your desires are given to you by God for you to choose to accept or reject. They are inherited through covenant with the one who is one with you. You have *the mind of Christ*.

1 Corinthians 2:11-16, "11 For who knows a person's thoughts except their own spirit within them? In the same way, no one knows the thoughts of God except the Spirit of God. 12 What we have received is not the spirit of the world, but the Spirit who is from God, so that we may understand what God has freely given us. 13 This is what we speak, not in words taught us by human wisdom but in words taught by the Spirit, explaining spiritual realities with Spirit-taught words. 14 The person without the Spirit does not accept the things that come from the Spirit of God but considers them foolishness, and cannot understand them because they are discerned only through the Spirit. 15 The person with the Spirit makes judgments about all things, but such a person is not subject to merely human judgments, 16 for, 'Who has known the mind of the Lord so as to instruct him?' But we have the mind of Christ."

The Holy Spirit gives us access to the mind of Christ. The Spirit knows the thoughts of God, for it is God, and we have received the same Spirit of God. Therefore our thoughts have been and are continually being transformed into his thoughts. That is why the command to lose your life is so prevalent. The quicker you can let go of your life with your control, the quicker you can have an ear to hear his life with his control.

Your dreams do not originate with you; they originate with God. They are insights into what he had written in his book before one of your days came to be (*Psalm 139:16*). Therefore, who has the authority to carry out a dream? Authority comes from the word author. It is acting as the originator in the original Latin sense. If your dreams originated with God, he has to be the one to enact them as the author. Since you are not the originator but a partner in a dream's working, the only risk for you is saying no. You do not risk by saying yes to your dreams; you only risk by saying no.

False security is a cause-and-effect way of thinking that we create when we, in a false allusion of control, build what we define as a safe life because we determine it has no risk. Let us break this down to understand what I am getting at in this chapter and book, fully.

Control is relative. The only thing we control is our free-willed yes or no to God's plan. When we give him a usual yes, we have no issue with the thought of not being in control because we find comfort and safety under the *shadow of his wings*. However, when we give him a usual no, it can look like we are creating a life for ourselves because we have rejected the life he created for us so many times. As stated in a previous chapter, the only image in creation is God's. Anything other than God's image is a mask; it is not real.

When we turn from God and his plans, we do not drift into another world of our creating but a nothingness abyss. Nothingness can wear a mask of reality but behind the mask is an empty longing to be something that you can only find in the Creator. Before God's creative reasoning in *Genesis*, the world was void and formless, with darkness covering the deep. Reality apart from God is comparable. His creativity did not stop in *Genesis*. The universe is ever-expanding to this day. Creation is still in the process of responding to God's creative design. That design found its climax in you and I. God's masterpiece was humanity.

Safety is also relative. Feeling safe is simply feeling comfortable. Comfortability happens, typically, through time. The more time you spend in an environment, the more comfortable or safe you feel in that environment. Here again, you can feel safe in the abyss of Godless control if you spend enough time there. Ironically, that place is not safe at all. That is the danger of our modern idea of dreaming. We identify as safe and risk-free the most unsafe and risky reality we could entertain: a path God did not lay.

Our dreams are God's nudges to stay on his path. If it starts to feel risky, that does not mean there is a legitimate risk; it just means our idea of risk needs reforming. Philosophy and theology have to be married. If we process the correct information through a broken processing system, we always get broken results. We have to have the correct information and the proper processing system to get the right results. We have the correct information in the sense that we, no matter how old or young, have dreams living on the front of our thoughts that most of us have ignored. What we may lack is an exemplary processing system, aka, the right way of thinking.

If you think of your dreams as wishful thinking that the grass is greener on the other side, you will never pursue anything and will be another average religious box-checker. We do not need more of those. Those are the ones ruining the good ones. However, if you start to see your dreams as manifestations of God-given destiny, you will start to see risk in not following rather than following.

You also have to check at the door what I address many times in this book: expected outcome. Often what you think pursuing your dreams will produce is different than what they deliver. When that happens, you will see yourself as a failure, you will doubt God's call in the first place, and you will stop saying yes to his whispers, if you judge success on your standard rather than his.

This covenant is all or nothing. To reiterate, Jesus says in *Matthew 6:39 TPT, " All who seek to live apart from me will lose it all. But those who let go of their lives for my sake and surrender it all to me will discover true life!"*

Dreamers are the ones who have committed to the life of trust. They are the ones who say, "whatever comes my way, no matter the outcome or cost, as long as I get you in the end, I trust you. I give you an unconditioned yes and choose to follow where you lead for you are the only way, truth, and life." Dreamers will constantly challenge the status quo. They live in a peace that no one understands. While the world is crumbling around those "safe" people in the culture, they are the ones standing firm, planted by streams of living water that bear fruit in every season. Their trust in the faithfulness of God will be all the confirmation needed to take the road less traveled.

Being a dreamer is popular phraseology today. Everyone wants to "follow their dreams." I am not talking about the apathetic approach to dreaming. I am talking about a radical yes to what "*no eye has seen, no ear has heard, and no mind has comprehended*" (*1 Corinthians 2:9*). When we started our church in 2017, we used to tell people we were taking a "big step of faith." The Lord corrected me later and said that every step in the walk of the beloved ones should be a step of faith. It is not out of the ordinary, and it is not uncertain, as the connotation might suggest. It is the natural next step in the journey.

Do not make a Goliath out of a blessing. I am not saying following your dreams, as the Lord gives them, is going to be naturally easy, especially in the beginning stages. What I am saying is once you are truly convinced that God is so good that he finds his absolute joy in what he can give his kids, you will start seeing your dreams as hints to where his gifts are hiding for you rather than a dare to gamble failure.

Then, dreaming will not be rare; it will be the way of life for the family of believers. Imagination will be what defines the generation that fulfills the prayer for God's kingdom to come on earth as it is in heaven. I believe once you start leveraging your imagination to image things into the nation (or the environment around you), you will start praying prayers you never prayed before your imagination filled them.

God not only wants to meet us at our level of imagination and dreaming, but he also, according to *Ephesians 3:20*, wants to exceed our level. *Matthew 7:2b* says, " *with the measure you use, it will be measured to you.*" Our level of yes will determine our level of authority to see our dreams come to pass. That is our destiny: a continual series of yeses to the one who laid the path of our lives.

The words *it is finished* unleashed God's creative nature to revive our inner likeness so that as God's words, that originated in his imagination, called creation into existence, our words, that originate in our imagination and dreams, can call creation into originality. It all comes full circle, and it all depends on how much we trust that God gives.

Dream again.

CHAPTER 9

WHISPERING WARRIOR

———— ✦ ◆ ✦ ————

Spiritual warfare has been a popular topic among evangelicals over the past decade. We are always swinging swords at the devil and dodging his. Warfare indicates two opposing sides are fighting against each other, both with an opportunity to be victorious. The devil wins on some (or most) days, and we win on the days we happen to muster ourselves to hope and peace in the Holy Spirit.

The greatest warrior in the history of Israel was, to me at least, Queen Esther. The Lord placed her in a position (as Queen) to speak on behalf of the Israelites. She shifts their destiny from total death to fully alive with their enemy defeated by the words of her mouth. She never lifted a sword and never rode into battle; she saved a nation by her whisper. God gifted Esther authority and made her warfare a matter of intimacy with the king rather than battlefield proficiency.

So many Christians are failing at spiritual warfare today because they are swinging swords rather than boldly approaching the throne of grace to make their requests known. Paul writes an interesting piece of imagery about warfare that has often gotten misinterpreted in *Ephesians 6*. He says:

> *11 Put on all of God's armor so that you will be able to stand firm against all strategies of the devil. 12 For we are not fighting against flesh-and-blood enemies, but against evil rulers and authorities of the unseen world, against mighty powers in this dark world, and against evil spirits in the heavenly places.*
>
> *13 Therefore, put on every piece of God's armor so you will be able to resist the enemy in the time of evil. Then after the battle you will still be standing firm. 14 Stand your ground, putting on the belt of truth and the body armor of God's righteousness. 15 For shoes, put on the peace that comes from the Good News so that you will be fully prepared. 16 In addition to all of these, hold up the shield of faith to stop the fiery arrows of the evil one. 17 Put on salvation as your helmet, and take the sword of the Spirit, which is the Word of God.*

The belt is truth, the armor is righteousness, the shoes are peace, the shield is faith, the helmet is salvation, the sword is the Word of God. Now, you tell me how many of those would be helpful in battle? None. Of course, Paul is using imagery. The question is, for what is he giving us this imagery?

Truth, righteousness, peace, faith, salvation, and the Word of God, are all identifying qualities of a born again son or daughter. Because of the incarnation, you are a coheir with Christ (*Romans 8:17*), seated on the throne with Christ (*Ephesians 2:6*), and joined as one with Christ (*1 Corinthians 6:17*). The ability to stand firm against all the enemy's strategies is knowing fully who you are and where you are seated, not getting down in the dirt with the devil.

Distraction comes in all forms and fashions, but the primary distraction we face is the one that does not look distracting at all. How much do we miss in establishing God's kingdom if all we ever do is fight an already defeated pip-squeak? Understand what I said: already defeated. If the Kansas City Chiefs won the Super Bowl and two days later started practicing again for the Super Bowl that they already played and won, you would call them crazy. They should not be practicing to play a game they already played and won; they should be planning a celebration parade as champions.

Jesus defeated every power of darkness on the cross, dethroned sin's monarch, and undid Adam's fall. Our job is not to defeat the powers of darkness that Christ already defeated but to establish Christ's victory to the ends of the earth. Fighting to win and establishing a win is very different yet can be very similar if we are unaware of our faith's pure orthodoxy.

Spiritual warfare, as taught and known today, is dangerous. It has spread into every denomination and every upbringing. On average, it takes around 20 to 30 years to establish a widely accepted theological belief in the church. There has to be the conception of an idea, a scholarly review, a scholarly acceptance, and a shift in how we teach this particular belief or view in higher education. Next, correctly taught students must occupy the roles of pastor and teacher in churches, and congregants must hear this new idea taught through regular instruction.

Teachings like the rapture and our current understanding of spiritual warfare will probably be laid to rest, finally, when I retire. However, I hope to expedite the process by being transparent through mediums like the book you are currently reading.

Having said all of this, it does not matter how grounded in historical and biblical truth an idea is; the one thing that people cannot seem to get past in the American Church as a whole is the obstacle of how they grew up.

I never want to degrade the lessons I learned growing up in church. Maturing in belief is not dishonoring what you believed before; it is honoring what you believed before as a stepping stone to get you to a level you would have never been without that piece of your journey. Thank God, though, we have evolved in our revelation of so much that we must have the grace to both receive and let the Holy Spirit reform when needed. It is incredible how valid the words of Jesus are when he says, *"wide is the gate and broad is the way that leads to destruction and many find it" (Matthew 7:13).* What you see in terms of God's kingdom is directly determined by how much you trust him when he comes to edit the misunderstandings in our belief systems. He is not concerned with what most of the Church believes or learned growing up; he is concerned with the Church living on true north.

Jesus got killed because what he taught was so much more profound in understanding than what the majority grasped, that they considered it wrong. The widespread belief about the teachings of Jesus was that they were demonic and crazy. However, Jesus was the very Word of God they were using to try and prove he was wrong. I wonder how much the Lord is trying to teach the Church today that we call wrong because the Church refuses to submit to revision when needed. We need to have discernment for false teaching now more than ever. I am not talking about false teaching in general; I am talking about orthodox teaching rejected because it is deeper than the shallow end of the theological pool where we have spent our whole lives.

It is shallow to swing swords with the devil. That will get a crowd roaring for battle and giving to help the cause. That does not make it right, and if you spend your life swinging a sword, you will live burned out and wondering why you keep getting your teeth kicked in. It is because you were never designed to be a sword swinger. You were designed to receive victory through Jesus. As his image-bearer, seated with him with the same power that raised him from the dead, you are to establish his victory in every inch of creation.

David wanted to build a permanent home for the Lord, but the Lord would not allow him to because he had too much blood on his hands. He never learned to lay down the sword for a mantle of peace. However, the Lord did allow Solomon, whose name means peace, to build a permanent home for the Lord (*1 Chronicles 28:2-7*). The Lord desires habitations where his presence can rest permanently on cities and nations. Nevertheless, he will not allow people who continually feel the need to shed the blood of spiritual warfare to be his habitation. He is looking for a people so rooted in peace that they know their words have a power their swords never will.

It is no surprise that prayer is at an all-time low in Christians today. We are the least praying generation of Christians in history. Prayer takes trust. Prayer takes believing in your identity and his identity. We lack all of those qualities and are not taught, for the most part, those qualities, so we have replaced authentic authority that only comes through prayer with the fake version of authority that you can extort through exerted effort. The Church is not losing steam in the world; it is gaining like never before in nations where persecution is everywhere. The Church in the West is in a season of fruitlessness because God loves us too much to let us think we can spread the gospel through our best effort.

The well-known phrase we use today is the Church "experience." We want people to be comfortable and have a good time. However, we are not selling an experience; we are hosting the presence of almighty God. You cannot buy and sell the real thing. The real thing will only rest on those who have ceased their efforts and committed to such a level of peace that they can receive. I can genuinely say I am convinced that my whispers impact the cosmos more than my anger at the devil. I am not saying being mad at the devil is wrong, but I am saying we need to stop giving all of our attention to a defeated cockroach. The devil is not making you look at porn or steal money from God; you make that decision as a creature in authority. You do not need a 12 step program to teach you that at any point, you can say no, and it all ceases.

Did you know that temptation is as simple as you saying yes or no? There is no gun to your head saying, "do this, or I shoot." It is you, in complete authority, saying yes to something you were not made for. This reality is excellent news! If you can say yes, you can say no. You have this capability because of what Jesus did on the cross. He gave you the authority back. You are not trying to get authority from the prominent ruler called satan; you are leveraging your authority as a son and daughter of God.

The earth is crying out for whispering warriors whose weapon of choice is proximity to the king. I was taught years ago by a spiritual father that our yes to Jesus results in a no to every other inferior thing. Rather than saying no, no, no, to every evil thought, give a never-ending yes to Jesus. Could our focus on the feet of our king cause us to hunger and thirst for something far greater than the quick fix of temptation's call? I think so. That is my story.

Every day I wake up early before the sun comes up. I go to my dining room table, turn on a lamp, grab a cup of fresh coffee, and spend an hour or two with Jesus (depending on how long my daughter sleeps in). Sometimes that looks like a deep study of scripture, sometimes that looks like journaling, and sometimes it looks like silently waiting. However, every morning that time results in a taste for something sin could never satisfy. Maybe that is what David meant when he dared us to *"taste and see that the Lord is good."* He believed one taste would be enough to realign the whole of our appetite to long for the king. I concur from experience that this has been the case.

I used to crave being stalwart in the battle against the enemy. Now I crave being so close to the king that my whispers shift nations. C.S. Lewis wrote, "Aim at heaven, and you will get earth thrown in. Aim at earth, and you will get neither." No more profound words have ever left the pen of one of the world's most impactful writers. Within them lies the key to life. Aim at Jesus, and you get everything else as a cherry on top. Aim at anything other than Jesus, and you get nothing. Do not aim your focus on the devil; aim your focus on Jesus.

Lean on God as a giver. Victory is not earned or achieved; it is received. Turn up your prayer life with fresh fuel that your words are not just bouncing up to the ceiling and back to the earth empty. Your words are putting seeds into the creation that will grow into his kingdom come. Jesus lovers are the foundation of the new creation. His army is an army of lovers, so smitten with the one they love, that he is willing to give them the nations at their request. Your whispers matter. We need more whispers and fewer swings of the sword. You swing swords of spiritual warfare at your enemy. You whisper love secrets and desires to your beloved. Shifting to the latter makes all the difference.

How do we do spiritual warfare? We put on the belt of truth, the armor of righteousness, the shoes of peace, the shield of faith, the helmet of salvation, and the sword of the Word of God. Our weapon is the promises that God has already spoken. I have victory not because I earned it by resisting temptation but because he told me he has already won the victory for me. I resist temptation by receiving the reward of my yes: total victory.

Now is the time for us to open our belief system and get a massive boost to our Christology. The more you know and learn about your king, and the more you draw close to your king, the more you will settle for the gentle whispers of inherited victory. You never struggle with burnout when all you do is receive at his feet.

> Psalm 1:1-3 TPT, "1 What delight comes to the one who follows God's ways! He will not walk in step with the wicked, nor share the sinner's way, nor be found sitting in the scorner's seat. 2 His pleasure and passion is remaining true to the Word of 'I Am,' meditating day and night in the true revelation of light. 3 He will be standing firm like a flourishing tree planted by God's design, deeply rooted by the brooks of bliss, bearing fruit in every season of his life. He is never dry, never fainting, ever blessed, ever prosperous."

CHAPTER 10

PAIN AND
DISAPPOINTMENT

❦

Being encouraged in what God gives is, of course, the premise of this book. However, some of you (maybe most of you) reading this book have probably had thoughts about why you have had to face the things you have faced in life if God is so generous. While I am not qualified to answer the problem of pain and suffering sufficiently, I would like to offer some thoughts on the matter.

Pain and disappointment are major dams built to keep God's generous goodness from flowing down our lives. Sometimes we build those dams; other times, they are built for us. We often believe that with every measure of goodness comes another measure of disappointment. Even if that disappointment is not from God, we would rather live mundane and whole (whatever you define whole as) than edgy with the possibility of getting broken.

I am reminded of the words of Jesus when he promised that *in this world we would have trouble* in *John 16:33.* Here is the tension of being in between new creation and current creation. We partner with Jesus to bring his kingdom into the earth, but until it comes in its fullness, we are in between worlds, if you will. One of my favorite quotes on pain is from C.S. Lewis' book *The Problem of Pain.* He says, "God whispers to us in our pleasures, speaks in our conscience, but shouts in our pains: it is His megaphone to rouse a deaf world."

There are many moving parts to the cause of pain and disappointment. One is free will. Reformed thinkers and non-reformed thinkers like to argue whether we live in a predestined reality or a free-willed reality. I do not think it matters and do not see it being taught or concerned one way or the other in scripture. Both are present, and both are needed. We have free will, and God is also sovereign, all at the same time. We do not have to know how or why; we only have to understand that this is what scripture teaches, and the rest we will have to trust the Lord through.

Humans were given great authority in creation. *Psalm 8:6* declares about humanity, "*You made them rulers over the works of your hands; you put everything under their feet."* Humans are the authority over the creation. This government works when we are under the authority of the Creator. However, with great authority comes great responsibility, as the movies rightly say, which is one of the reasons why the Lord gives the Old Testament law and all of its seeming strict policies. They were not to hold us back; they were to align us in a place where we could, in the words of *Genesis 1*, subdue or govern the earth.

When we use this authority in conjunction with a covenantal relationship with Jesus, it calls creation into its original design by bringing glimpses of the new creation into our current day. When we use this authority for evil, it brings chaos. God was okay trusting man with authority, knowing some would use it in the wrong way. It would throw the whole system out of order for the Lord to step in and change every wrong decision and let live every correct decision. That is no longer free will, and we, in theory, would no longer have the authority to govern the creation we were assigned to govern. Because of this, God does not step in and change our every wrong decision when it happens. Instead, he redeems every wrong decision for good.

You may ask, "what is the difference?" By God allowing us to make free-willed decisions, it causes us to grow, learn, and ultimately partner with him as he desires. Nothing grows you more than the aftermath of a wrong decision. Nothing refines your understanding of a correct decision more than a realized wrong one. Therefore the Lord gives us room to fall on our own but does not leave us there. He falls with us so that he can pick us up and set us back in our rightful place after we fail. That is the beauty and the mystery of free will. My goal is not to dive deep into free will theory. Instead, I long to give you tiny road maps of thinking paths that maybe you have never been down.

I am thankful the Lord gives us the free will and authority to make decisions. In my own past, when I did not lean on the Holy Spirit (more on this in a moment), some of my worst decisions led to the greatest gifts in my life. For example, my posture for being in ministry was that I wanted to be a famous worship leader. The thinking behind that decision was off. However, the Lord redeemed that line of thinking by allowing me to meet my wife, have a daughter with my wife, and ultimately start a church family that is finding what it means to live life to the full. I would not be where I am today had it not been for some bad decisions. I am not sanctioning immoral decisions, but I am trying to give you a picture of how the Lord works with us. If he had stopped my bad decisions, I would not be in the *good* I am in today. He does not stop them; he redeems them.

Covenant and being filled with the Holy Spirit now start to make much more sense when you understand our lives' significance in governing creation. Because my decisions carry weight, the Lord fills me with the Holy Spirit (or the Spirit of Wisdom) due to my becoming one with Jesus. The more I lean into the understanding of the Spirit of God, the more I begin to make the decisions the Spirit would make rather than the ones I would make. I start to see things differently, my perspective is higher, and I minimize my failings because I am not leaning on my own understanding, as I did before my covenant with Jesus, but I am leaning on his understanding and how Jesus sees things. He has partnered with us to bring his kingdom into the earth. Accordingly, he fills us with what fills him.

> *1 Corinthians 2:10b-13, "10 ...The Spirit searches all things, even the deep things of God. 11 For who knows a person's thoughts except their own spirit within them? In the same way no one knows the thoughts of God except the Spirit of God. 12 What we have received is not the spirit of the world, but the spirit who is from God, so that we may understand*

*what God has freely given us. 13 This is what we
speak, not in words taught us by human wisdom but
in words taught by the spirit, explaining spiritual
realities with Spirit-taught words."*

Now, back to the effects of free will on our pain and
disappointment. Unfortunately, sometimes humans
use free will in despicable ways. Rape, abuse, murder,
and the like are all too prevalent in our society. I do not
want to gloss over these but face them head-on. These
are fundamental questions people have that usually
get avoided because there is a gap in understanding.
The Old Testament and New Testament alike are filled
with atrocities. The first murder is found just four
chapters into the Bible. In the New Testament early
church, leaders got beheaded, burned alive, crucified
upside down, and pulled apart by horses. Jesus himself
suffered brutally at the hands of men. Evil is nothing
new. It has been a part of our story since the first act
of disobedience in *Genesis 3*. Why, though, does God
allow it?

First, I would say he does not allow evil as we
think of him allowing evil. When we ask why God
allows something, what we are asking is why God
sanctions it. There are subtle hints of us thinking God
possibly even wanted evil to happen when we think

of him allowing an act or acts to take place. After 9/11, people questioned God. After the holocaust, people questioned God. After the 2008 financial crisis, people questioned God. Throughout those tragedies and others, the common thread is that there is a human, or many humans, behind the perilous decisions that became world-changing moments. Understanding the authoritative role humans have been given in creation, I would not ask why God allowed something to happen. Instead, I would ask why humans, behind those bad decisions, allowed something to happen.

In typical fashion, we blame ourselves for all the good in the world and God for all the bad. We do not question God when good things happen, only when bad things happen. I believe this is because we do not want to take the difficult journey of rediscovering what humanity has in its DNA. There is a unifying quality in every person: we are all made in the image and likeness of God. Evangelism is essential not because we need to get everyone out of this old wretched world, but because we need to carry the transformation of the globe we are in charge of to those who aren't living in the image and likeness they were made in.

You may have a past marred by bad decisions that you did not choose. God knows every tear you have cried and has them in a jar for redemption. He promises to take everything the enemy meant for evil and use it for your good. God also promises to work all things, good and bad, together for the good of those who love (or prefer) God. In the end, the hope of our salvation is Jesus, and when he returns, resurrection and justice will flow completely throughout creation. If you have a complicated past that has shackled you in a distant position from God, I encourage you to allow God to do what he longs to do: redeem it.

The blessing and curse of free will is that we are free to will. We love free will on the mountain and hate it in the valley. However, it is God's vehicle for bringing redemption into the cosmos. The fact that there is a mystery surrounding ideas like free will is not an invitation to doubt but an invitation to trust. I love that the Lord leaves me in a world of mystery. It allows me to sit at his feet and enjoy the peace of knowing he has everything figured out for me rather than trying to figure everything out on my own. Trust is beautiful if you can ever leverage it.

What about the pain and disappointment that free will cannot explain? Pandemics, earthquakes, hurricanes, and everything in between are not the fruit of a decision but are nature in chaos. Free-willed evil is the result of humanity's decisions. Nature's chaos is the result of humanity's dilusion that it is far from God. In the Old Testament, we see plagues, earthquakes, and the like were sent by God when God's people turned away from exclusivity to the one they were with in covenant. Within the intimate proximity of covenant, there was protection from the spinning of an unredeemed nature. Outside of proximity, that protection was invalid.

I will get some pushback for this line of thinking, but it is biblical and trustworthy. *Romans 8:19* says, "*For the creation waits in eager expectation for the children of God to be revealed.*" The Greek word for *revealed* is the title of the last book of the Bible (*Revelation*): *apokalupsis*. It means uncovering, unveiling, revealing, or revelation. There are many hints to the reality of the Garden of Eden in this. What happened when Adam and Eve sinned? They realized they were naked and covered their nakedness. What is creation waiting for in eager expectation? You and I to be so convinced of our identity and proximity with God that we remove the cover that once hid our shame and become the bride who has removed her veil. We have no shame at the feet of Jesus. Shame is what Jesus took on our behalf, and the exchange he offers is for us to live, now and forever, unashamed.

Why is creation awaiting this? The rest of this section in *Romans 8* reads:

> *20 For the creation was subjected to frustration, not by its own choice, but by the will of the one who subjected it, in hope 21 that the creation itself will be liberated from its bondage to decay and brought into the freedom and glory of the children of God.*

Humanity's fall from design caused creation's frustration (or chaos), but creation is anticipating our return to design because when we are out of place, creation is out of place; when we are in our rightful place, creation is too. To summarize, as we go, so goes creation. This is key to understanding evil or "bad things" that cannot be explained by free will. We live in a world with image-bearers who have not been unveiled of God yet. Because of that, we also live in a world that has not been redeemed to its original state yet.

The question is not why God allows terrible things to happen. There are mysteries we are going to live with until we see Jesus face-to-face. That is a good thing. The book of *James*, in *chapter one*, says, "*the testing of our faith ultimately makes us mature and complete, lacking nothing*" (summarized). Therefore mystery invokes testing.

Testing invokes opportunities to exercise trust, which makes us lack nothing, causing us to live unveiled, as who we are: sons and daughters. The Eastern way of thinking (the Bible was written as an Eastern book) is to take what you are given and allow that to continually grow and shape you into the person you are intended to be. There is not much questioning how or why. It is simply trusting that if "how" or "why" has been withheld, it must not be necessary. Trust is the first response, not the last resort.

In the West, we want to know what the equation equals and the perfect understanding of everything we encounter. This craving goes directly against the biblical agenda in numerous ways. The whole foundation of a covenant is trust. If I know the one I am married to, I do not have to know all the details of everything they do. I know they have my best interest at heart, so I can live worry-free in the reality that no matter what they are doing, it is for my good. I say this because for us to try and answer where sicknesses or hurricanes come from, and why, is never going to produce a perfect answer. That is okay. It does not need to. We were given the blueprint to host God's kingdom on the earth until we see its realized fullness in the restored creation.

Beyond the shadow of a doubt, the things we do know are that our proximity is the first step to creation's freedom from decay, we have been given the authority over creation to begin to call it into order, and humans in chaos will always breed a creation in chaos. We are on offense. We need to begin to tell things of creation what they are rather than bracing for what they are telling us they are. We need to begin caring for the globe as if it is our responsibility because it is. Why can't we speak to rivers and sing to flowers? The frequency that is leaving our identity is what they are all waiting for, in eager expectation.

Pain and disappointment cannot be fully explained or understood; for like time (see next chapter), it is relative to the individual experiencing it. What I call pain and disappointment you may not think is painful or disappointing at all. We must see above the here and now, or then and there, and into the glorious destiny of what God has planned for us. I cannot give you all the answers to why things have happened to you. I can promise you that all of it will be worked for your good as you trust and prefer his ways above your own. I can give you some tools to stop focussing on the bad that has happened in your life and start focussing on the good coming from your life. You are God's image-bearer. You are one of his perfect creatures in humanity. When God looks at you, he does not see you as your past, what you have done, or what others have labeled you as. He sees you as the one he designed in your mother's womb. Only one gets to give you your name, and his name is Yahweh.

Pain and disappointment are like shackles in an open prison. The doors are open for you to run free, but you are still chained down. The great news is Jesus give us the key to unlock the shackles. Take the key and run out of the prison that has kept you from receiving goodness from his hand. God is generous and is ready to pour out a blessing that has been pressed down, shaken together, and is running over for those who have given up all the inferior things in their hands and have approached him empty but open. When you create space, God delights in filling it.

CHAPTER 11

RIGHT ON TIME

Have you ever heard the phrase, "he may not come when you want him, but he will be there right on time?" When it comes to God's timing, this kind of thinking is correct in a sense, but an inadequate way of looking at timing in its entirety.

Timing is relative. Who you are, what your experiences have been, and your trust in God will always determine what you see as *on time*. To the one who has walked with God their whole lives, a year or two is nothing to wait on a promise God spoke. To the new Christian, a day feels like a century, and often, they will start grasping at the first thing that looks remotely close to what God said, even if it is not at all what he meant.

Because our timing is shifty, to say the least, we must do as we have done throughout this book: redefine what we see as time altogether. If we try to fit

God's infinite, eternal clock onto our 24-hour clock, we are going to get chaos. The easiest thing to do is to try and get God to submit to what we want, when we want it. It should come as no surprise that this only leads to disappointment and compromise. Here is where the majority of the Church finds herself today. We have told God how we want things to look, what we want them to accomplish, and when we want them done. Then, because that is not how this covenant works, we try to play God's role and start answering our own prayers because how he is responding to them is not good enough.

Tell me, and I do not mean to offend anyone with this but, did we ever sit in a quiet room and ask God if he wanted us to turn his house into a weekly rock show? Did we ask God if he wanted us to reach people with free giveaways? Did we ask God if he wanted us to make his bride a franchise model organization that mimicked the latest business trends? Or did we assume that is how the church is supposed to spread the good news because it is relevant, what is working for our culture, and what attracts "unbelievers?"

To answer for you, we assumed. While coming from a pure heart, what we have essentially said is, "God, you are not enough, but I read a business book, and now I am going to step in and save your empty-seated, stain-glassed church by becoming relevant." We traded the presence of God for the masses' attendance. Now, we have a culture full of packed churches and more misplaced kids than ever before.

Our current Church culture results from trying to get God to bend to our will and our time and always taking control when we think God is lazy. Therefore, we do not need to redeem the current model; we need to throw away the current model and resurrect the one we buried because it took too long and was not *cool enough*.

The early Church generations were content playing their individual, God-designed piece of the master plan to redeem creation. They had eyes on the new creation and resurrection, and, because of that, they were not in a hurry. They trusted that God had everything figured out.

2 Peter 3:8, "...With the Lord, a day is like a thousand years and a thousand years are like a day..."

God does not think in terms of time; he thinks in terms of readiness. We would rather have something quick and wrong than slow and correct. However, for

God, all he cares about is doing things right. The reason we are not seeing the outpouring of the Presence of God right now is that God knows if he did pour out his Spirit on what we have built, we would take the credit for it and continue deeper into our organizational mindsets. He would rather wait a thousand years, if that is what it took, for us to realize we are not here for a show; we are here for his feet.

Repentance has never been more relevant than in the current topic. God will not redeem your handmade box, but he will invite you into his. I wonder if we thought we were building God's Church in the past two generations while we were actually destroying it? It takes guts and immense trust in God's goodness to change how we think, but it is vital if we are going to play our part in the new creation project.

King David had two sons in line to be king after him who got tired of waiting for the anointing to the throne and tried to make themselves king. They both ended up dead. David had one son that initially was not in line to be king but inherited the kingship by way of proximity to home and a willingness to wait for the appointed time. Not only did he become king, but he also ended up building the dwelling place of God with God's people. He developed the place of *on earth as it is in heaven.*

Why do we struggle so much with timing? I believe the root cause is poverty in the secret place. When you have aligned yourself with the one thing (*see Psalm 27:4*), time suddenly becomes irrelevant. You have everything you want in the place where you meet your beloved and dwell together. The more I spend time with Jesus, the less I care about all the things I used to care about that benefitted my "calling." I actually find myself redefining my calling entirely. Today, when someone asks me what I feel called to do, I say, "be with him."

It is in this place where you can start inheriting things in his timing that you never let yourself inherit before when you were mad that God was not operating on your timing. Does God want to transform our cities? Absolutely. However, if God transformed our cities before transforming his Church in our cities, what would happen? You would have an outbreak of spiritual homelessness. It would be inadequate, in my opinion, for millions of people to get saved in America right now because they would be invited into retail religion rather than authentic covenant. Religion ends in death. Covenant makes death illegal.

If we fixed the wineskin of the church, we would inherit the wine of the world transformed effortlessly.

If we have to strive to find the lost, it is because we do not carry enough Presence in our lives to find the lost. Finding the lost should be as simple as walking into a restaurant and eating and the Presence streaming off of you saying more than a 30-minute sermon could ever say. That understanding is not popular because we are so used to working hard for it. Although, Jesus never worked hard for anything in ministry. Moreover, if Jesus did not, why would we? Jesus received those who would call on the name of the Lord through his relationship with the Father. Since we are now one with that same Jesus, we have to seriously start asking why our lives look so different from his.

Jesus' ministry ended with 120 in an upper room. Not thousands, not hundreds, but 120. Was this a successful ministry? Yes. Jesus would do more with 120 authentic ones than thousands of religious posers. The globe has changed due to those 120 in covenant. Nevertheless, it took 2,000 years to get where we are now. In the current culture, we would have left that upper room on day two and started telling everyone we could about how Jesus called a dead Lazarus out of a tomb. That would have caused a crowd to stir, but in a couple of generations, it would have fizzled out. The only thing that causes longevity in the Church is Presence. Their stories are not what drew 3,000 people on the day of Pentecost to them; their fire was what drew 3,000 people. Then, guess what those 3,000 people took back to their homes? Not stories; fire.

God operates on what I like to refer to as *timelessness*. That is to say, God's only objective is the healthy delivery of what he spoke. Healthy delivery is determined by when God desires to release us and when we are ready to receive. The verse directly after *2 Peter 3:8*, which I quoted before, says this:

> *2 Peter 3:9, "The Lord is not slow in keeping his promise, as some understand slowness. Instead, he is patient with you, not wanting anyone to perish, but everyone to come to repentance."*

Of course, these two verses are in the middle of Peter talking about the return of Christ, but the revelation behind them concerns timing. He says the Lord is not slow. Instead, he is patient. Until writing this chapter, I never caught that. I have read *2 Peter* many times, considering it is only three chapters long, but I never stopped to think about how I should see time differently when I begin to understand that God is never slow, but he is ever patient. The difference is that *slow* carries an apathetic and somewhat lazy energy. When I say you are slow, what I am saying is that you are lazy. Then, to go a step deeper, once you have convinced yourself that God's being lazy, you must start to believe he does not care enough to give it his total energy.

Patience, however, carries precise, purposeful energy. Rather than acting immediately, patience is waiting for the right moment because it cares. What is slow is determined by a measurement of time. What is patient is determined by acting on and with purpose. Eternity is full of the essence of patience. Time is full of things happening fast or slow. I would argue that time has no capacity for patience because patience cannot be measured by time. When someone is operating in patience, a level of eternity that one has started to trust and live in must precede.

How would we see our lives differently if our idea of time, or lack thereof, was transformed? We would rejoice when God takes his time bringing something to pass because his patience means he cares. What is fighting against this transformation, particularly in younger generations, is social media. Projections abound in the lives and phones of most people 50 and younger. Those who would otherwise be more willing to trust the Lord's work are now itching for what is quick that looks like what everyone has and is doing.

As I said earlier in this chapter, we, as a society, no longer care about doing what is right; we only care about doing what gets us a quick fix. Rich people, for example, are sometimes the most depressed people on planet earth. They have everything they want yet are impoverished to what is needed, which has been thrown away to pursue what is wanted that they believe will give them purpose. It genuinely strips their real purpose away. I am not saying having money is wrong. I am not even talking about money. I am talking about pursuit. What time lens we use will determine what we pursue. If I am living and moving on a timed dimension, I want what is fast because time is always a depreciating asset. If I am living and moving on an eternal dimension, I want what is best because time is an appreciating asset.

The Church body needs to allow the Lord to give us his time. Eternity is an inheritance received from God. Time is an instrument we use to try and make something happen on our own (sometimes in the name of God). To go back to the phrase this chapter started with, I do not like, from a philosophical standpoint, the part that says, "when you want him." When I want him to act is irrelevant. It does not matter when I want him to do anything. We need to have the grace to receive *when* rather than conjuring it up on our own based on our unwillingness to be patient.

The irony is that we see ourselves as patient when we see God as slow. It is not God who needs to speed things up; we need to inherit a new clock. A clock void of numbers, lines, and arms. A clock that is a blank canvas waiting for the right colors, the right moment and the true purpose of identity to be brushed across its seeming nothingness, only to find that its void was only the patience of the artist plotting their grand design. Time and seasons were given to us to measure God's faithfulness, not short-circuit it.

Living in the moment and embracing what each day brings is waiting on the other side of tasting the patience of eternity. Entrance into the taste is the secret place of devotion where you become a holy of holies intersection between heaven and earth. Time stands still when the king of eternity enters the room. I often wonder if when Moses was on the mountain receiving the covenant, in *Exodus*, if those 40 days and nights felt like 40 days and nights or if, in the wonder of face-to-face communion, those many days felt like a moment.

In eternity, all moments past, present, and future are now. The story of creation in *Genesis* climaxes with Sabbath. Then, God's people are later commanded, in *Exodus 20:8-11, "8 Remember the Sabbath day by keeping it holy. 9 Six days you shall labor and do all your work, 10 but the seventh day is a sabbath to the Lord your God. On it, you shall not do any work, neither you, nor your son or daughter, nor your male or female servant, nor your animals, nor any foreigner residing in your towns. 11 For in six days, the Lord made the heavens and the earth, the sea, and all that is in them, but he rested on the seventh day. Therefore the Lord blessed the Sabbath day and made it holy."*

Jewish tradition states that the Sabbath was a glimpse of eternity. Sabbath is held in such high esteem because you should not miss the fleeting shadow of eternity in which you are resting. It is a day of timelessness. You do not feel the urge to toil, for, on the Sabbath, you recognize that everything you have is from the hand of God, not from the hand of man. When God commands the Israelites to *remember* the Sabbath, it is not to keep a memory of it for later, but to always keep it on the forefront of their minds. The more accurate understanding of *verse 8* is, *"The way you view everything in your life through the Sabbath is upholding its holiness above all other days."* Jesus reiterates this later in the New Testament when he teaches about seeking first the kingdom of God and his righteousness (*Matthew 6:33*). Not first in a priority list; first as in that being the thing you see everything thing else through. The Jews saw the idea of "first" not in a successive list but a circle. Seeking the kingdom of God and his righteousness would be the outer ring or layer of the circle that everything else found itself within.

In the old covenant, the Sabbath was a day; in the new covenant, the Sabbath is a lifestyle. You cannot live in timelessness until you rest, and you cannot rest until you live in timelessness. They go hand-in-hand. Today's juxtaposition is that we teach people to live in rest without teaching them that rest first requires a death to the clocked dimension where we have learned to live.

What does it mean to live in timelessness? What does life look like free from the clock? The answer is straightforward. It means you have a high trust in God to do and fulfill things when he determines it is right; not based on what year it is, how many years it has been since (fill in the blank), or where you are in life, but solely when he determines it is right. Freedom from the clock is freedom into devotion. Time is irrelevant when we have the one who makes time stand still.

CHAPTER 12

THE END

———— ◆◆◆ ————

Icannot write a book on the generosity of God without talking about eschatology. Eschatology means theology concerning the end. Let me start by giving this significant caveat: my view, and quite frankly the biblical view, of the end is presumably going to be different than how you grew up in the West. My current view is different than how I grew up. However, I encourage you to keep an open mind. We do not have to agree, and this could be food for thought for you. Having seen what I see as the truth, I cannot help but talk about it. This truth truly changes the entire playing field for God's kingdom in our midst. With that, buckle up.

I do not believe in the rapture. I believe, and the early Church believed, that Jesus is coming back to establish his kingdom in the new creation, not take us to a distant heaven. So, where did the rapture thinking come from if it did not originate in the early Church? Without writing a history book, I would love to give you a glimpse into why the rapture has become so widespread, particularly in the West.

As it is known, rapture theology originated in the 1830s with a man by the name of John Darby. He studied law at Westminster School and Trinity College. The Church of Ireland ordained him after he chose the ministerial path rather than law. His general theology was very shaky to the point that he rejected the idea of clergy because he said it limited the whole congregation from being led by the Holy Spirit. His shift in many views held tightly by the Church of Ireland caused Darby to split away from the church and start what would be known as the Plymouth Brethren. Around the time of this split, Darby began to formulate what we now know as rapture theology.

Because this belief had no scriptural basis and had never been taught by the Church before, this thinking was brand new and contrary to everything the Church had believed about the end since *Acts*. Darby based his thinking on one highly misinterpreted set of verses. The text is in *1 Thessalonians 4:15-17*.

*15 According to the Lord's word, we tell you that we who are still alive, who are left until **the coming*** *of the Lord, will certainly not precede those who have fallen asleep. 16 For the Lord himself will come down from heaven, with a loud command, with the voice of the archangel and with the trumpet call of God, and the dead in Christ will rise first. 17 After that, we who are still alive and are left will be **caught up** together with them in the clouds to meet the Lord in the air. And so we will be with the Lord forever.*

A quick look into the history of Thessalonica, the location of the group of people Paul is writing to, will reveal precisely what Paul is saying when he talks about *the coming* of the Lord. That word in Greek is *parousia*. The Thessalonicans would have been very familiar with this as they had this happen twice in the group's lifetime that received this letter.

Much of the Roman world was built along significant fault lines and because of this, they were susceptible to earthquakes. Because architecture was not then what it is today, a moderate earthquake could level a city. When this happened, the emperor would come to the city, assess the damages, and allocate money to rebuild the city. The only requirement in return for these resources was that they had to build the city back better than it was before.

After a while, the emperor would return (*parousia*) and assess what they had done with what he had left them. When he returned, there would be a blast of a trumpet, announcing the emperor was near, and everyone in the city would go out to meet the emperor outside of the city so that hand-in-hand, so to speak, they could walk in and show off their progress. If they were lazy and did nothing with the resources, they were severely punished. If they, say, built back the city and built a new arena named after the emperor with his statue in front to honor who gave them the resources to build back their city, they were commended. Not only that, Rome placed the graves of those who had died at the entrance of their cities. The first thing the emperor would do when coming into a city was pay homage to those who had gone before (or who had died).

If all of that sounds familiar, it is because it sounds exactly like what Paul wrote in *1 Thessalonians 4*. Remember, not only had this happened once for this group of people, it had happened twice. They knew Paul was writing to tell them to stop sitting on their lazy behinds waiting to get taken away and get to work stewarding the salvation resource Jesus had given them to partner with God in restoring his creation to originality. Jesus is not coming to take anyone away but to meet us "outside the city," so-to-speak, so that together we can walk into the new creation.

Now that we have established what this verse is genuinely saying let us revisit the rapture. John Darby started pushing what I call *escapism* until the 19th century, when CI Scofield picked up Darby's belief. Scofield had no theological training and self-gave himself the title of "D.D. or Doctor of Divinity." However, there is no record whatsoever of him ever earning a Doctor of Divinity degree. Later in life, Scofield abandoned his kids and wife to marry another woman. I do not ever want to be the one throwing darts at people's past. I do, though, need everyone to see the origins of the single belief guiding almost all other beliefs in the current American Church.

Scofield published one of the first widely used reference bibles in America and England and taught Darby's rapture in his bible's footnotes. Many held this bible as authoritative and therefore bought into the rapture belief system as Scofield wrote and Darby taught. That is the danger in us not being rooted in a secret place with the Lord. I do not want to believe what I believe because I read it in a reference bible; I want to believe what I believe because it is correct and orthodox.

American Christians are typically very gullible

to every wind of doctrine that blows through town. Christianity has become so religious that we care more about our grandparents' traditions than the first church's orthodoxy. While I hope generations to come can follow our traditions, and those remain orthodox because of the adjustments we are making now, for the most part, the generations that have gone before us have gotten this very wrong.

If I asked you if Jesus won the victory over everything, you would say yes. However, rapture thinking requires us to believe Jesus has to avoid darkness by snatching us up to float in a mystical heaven with a diaper and a harp on a cloud. Avoidance is not victory. Avoidance is defeat. Therefore, I believe I can chase rapture theology down the line until you get to the thinking that the Church will, even if for a season of "tribulation," get its teeth kicked in by the devil, whom we supposedly also believe is defeated.

If America goes to war with North Korea next month and in the heat of battle, we pack up our troops, bring them home, and let North Korea have its way, did we win that battle? No. Nevertheless, this is our current, Western, eschatology. I know this may be shocking to some of you, and you may have just closed the book and threw it in the garbage. If so, I love you, and so does Jesus. If you are still reading and you want to see the truth of what the bible teaches about the end, take a journey with me.

In *Genesis 3*, God moves Adam and Eve out of the Garden of Eden so that they wouldn't eat from the tree of life and make permanent their newly distorted identity. He placed them on the east of the Garden and placed a flaming sword and cherubim as guards of the tree of life. The later tabernacle faced east and had cherubim on the veil guarding the Holy of Holies. These are blatantly connected. The tree of life in the Garden of Eden was not to be off-limits forever. It was to be off-limits until humanity got its original image back.

When the Son of God, Jesus Christ, comes into the picture, John says he "pitched his tent" or "tabernacled" in us (*John 1:14*). Jesus is *the way, the truth, and the life* for us to get back to the tree of life, and by us finding our way back to the tree of life, it causes a chaotic creation to find its way back to its *good* identity. Adam and Even outside of the garden caused creation to move out of order and into chaos. Through Jesus, we find our way back to an inner garden that will cause creation to move back into order and reestablish its original intent.

The return of Jesus is when wickedness, not

righteousness, is totally and finally removed (*as in the days of Noah - Matthew 24:37*) from the creation, and Jesus establishes it fresh again, with us, in the new creation. There is two Greek words for new. There are *neos* which means newly created, and *kainos* which means fresh or brought back to original state. When John writes of seeing a *new heaven and new earth* in *Revelation 21:1*, he does not use the word for newly created (*neos*); he uses the word for, let us say, restored (*kainos*). That is interesting since the rapture thinking that most have held firm to for a hundred or so years has taught that the Lord wants to start over with a *new in age* creation. However, the bible teaches that God's plan all along was to restore his good creation and bring us, ultimately, back to the beginning.

The most famous verse in the bible is no doubt *John 3:16*. *John 3:17*, the verse directly after, is possibly more potent than the former. It says:

> *"God did not send his Son into the world to condemn the world, but to save the world through him."*

The world has become a well-known phrase nowadays for evil, particularly evil people. The Greek word for *the world* is *kosmos* which is where we get the English word cosmos. For the sake of simplicity, we can say that this word means *the creation*. Jesus came so that the entirety of his good creation, including man but not exclusive to man, would be saved (*sozo-* saved, healed, *rescued, or preserved*).

The difference between what I am teaching and what Darby and Scofield taught is that they were introducing something brand new that had never been taught or believed before. I, on the other hand, am simply teaching what the early Church always believed and taught. I am not introducing something new; I am reminding you of something original. Unfortunately, because of how far we have gone from the early Church, what they taught feels new when it is genuinely orthodox.

Now, you might be thinking to yourself, because I get this question a lot when teaching eschatology, "why does this matter?" In a book about God's generosity and how he is a giver by default, this matters immensely. Primarily, we have no grace to look beyond ourselves and our generation if we believe Jesus is coming to blow everything up and take us away any day now. I do not know when Jesus is coming back, and of course, it would be incredible if it was this afternoon. However, if you believe as the early Church believed about Jesus' return, you will have the grace to look hundreds of years ahead and make decisions today based on how it will affect your legacy.

In a nutshell, rapture theology destroys generations to come because it leaves no room to care for them. As a giver, though, God tells us he is planning a grand renewal that we will inherit at the coming of Jesus, and that we get to partner in his grand renewal, now, to bring it into the whole of the earth. He is not judging when to escape us by how prevalent evil is; he is judging when to give us the fullness of renewed creation by how we steward the measure we have now.

Chapter 13

Stewarding Generosity

O ne afternoon in early 2020, my family and I were on the way to buy some clothes for our daughter. As we pulled into the parking lot of one of the stores, I heard the Lord whisper, "you are going to lead the new holiness movement." Now, I grew up in a *holiness* environment, and it involved endless rules on what you could not wear, how you could not fix your hair, how you could not look, how you had to get rededicated to the Lord every time you sinned, and how you had to pretend to be perfect in front of church folk. Everyone called each other brother and sister, and we were not allowed to listen to any music with an electric guitar in it. My response to the Lord was not good. In that environment, I got "saved" tens of thousands of times because I was taught the most challenging thing in life was to "make it to heaven."

The enemy plays the Church. He does not tempt us to turn away from the truth; he gets us to buy into something that calls itself truth that's slightly left of actual truth. That moment of somewhat humor by the Lord led me on a journey to rediscovering what holiness is. I want to address the topic of holiness because holiness is not how you earn God's generosity; it is how you receive and steward it. For too long, we have made holiness the gateway into salvation. You have to do this in order to get that. By making it the gateway, we have been unable to utilize it correctly, which is in stewardship.

One of the prominent Greek words for holiness used in the New Testament is *hagiósuné* and it deals with the quality of being holy, sacred, set apart, or unique (one of a kind). It is an identifying word, not an action verb. Of course, what you are will always dictate what you do, but the root of holiness is the quality given to believers by God, specifically by the indwelling of the Holy Spirit. Living in holiness, therefore, cannot possibly be earned. Even if you were flawless in everything you did, you still would not earn holiness. It is a quality we receive. Think of this: God is so generous that even what he calls us to live in is *given* to us by him. He does not require works; he requires rest and open hands.

If holiness deals with a quality of our identity, how then should our lives look? In short, our lives should bear fruit, naturally, of who we are. You do not have to force having a good singing voice. You either have a good voice, or you do not. You do not have to force the ability to whistle. You either can or cannot (I cannot, by the way). You do not have to force what color your hair is (although some try). Your hair is the color it is naturally. You do not have to force holiness. You either are awakened to the truth that you are in Christ, and therefore holy, or you are not, yet.

There is maturity in holiness, just as there is in salvation. The more we mature in salvation and holiness, the more naturally we will bear fruit of holiness. Jesus did not have to make the conscious decision to be perfect. He was so solidified in his identity that it became impossible for him to bear fruit of a life that was anything but total holiness. We have made the topic of holiness behavior modification. I believe, and will present in this chapter, holiness is a two-fold root system that, when healthy, produces authentic holiness as fruit.

The first part of this root system deals with

reforming how we view holiness in general. There is a tension I want to live in throughout this chapter, and that is that holiness involves works yet is not earned by works. Let me say it like this: works can never produce holiness, but holiness will always produce works. Remember, we are talking about a quality, not an action. That is important because if we think of our works as a way to earn an identity, when our works inevitably fall short or fail, so will our identity. Here we find the reasoning behind why Western churches, like those that I grew up in, teach that you can lose your salvation frequently. When you see what you do as the building block for who you are, you build a house of cards that will fall at the slightest gust of wind.

It is dangerous to believe your works have that much authority over who you are. To believe that holiness is the sum of your works, you also have to believe salvation is a sum of your works. At that point, you strip the cross of its meaning, the resurrection becomes a cool blip in the history books, and believers trap themselves in an endless cycle of falling and getting back up. That describes the majority of believers' walks today. I do not say that to bash anyone; I do, nonetheless, say that to convict. Your works matter. They do not, however, matter in the way most think they matter. Your works matter because they tell the world who you are.

Let me use a parable of sorts.

There once was a student at a university with high aspirations to become an engineer. He had many books to read to pass his various classes. However, things were not working out, and he was failing each class.

When his professors began to dig into the student's grades, they could not figure out why a bright student like this one was doing so poorly. Then, one morning, his 10 AM class professor asked him, "why aren't you learning what the textbooks teach? You have got the correct books, right?"

"Yes, I have the right books," the student replied, "but each night I sit in my chair, open the books in front of me, and nothing happens. They will not teach me."

This is a funny example that is in your face with its meaning. That is the point. A book alone cannot teach you. Nevertheless, you can read a book and learn things, not simply because a book says it, but because you have the capability of processing and retaining information based on the intelligence of your brain. The words alone are worthless unless they meet a medium that processes the words into something useful. This parable is a picture of how holiness works.

If someone who was not born again lived perfectly, would they be living in holiness? No. Holiness is not what you produce; it is whom you become. Works will never produce holiness, but holiness will always produce works. Like the books in the story, works only have value when they meet the correct medium, which in this case is a holy identity. The works alone, though, cannot produce that which is holy.

When your works make up your identity, your identity is fluid. One day you believe you are righteous; the next day, you believe you are scum. We must remove these two from each other and put them in their proper place. Salvation (and identity) comes by Jesus alone. You cannot get it any other way but by receiving. When you separate identity from your works, you begin to do genuine works because you start to live in authentic identity.

How many generations have tried and failed to earn an identity that is only received or burned out their days trying to attain what is effortlessly inherited? The paradox is blatant. The Old Testament tells a story of rest, and every time humanity tries to effort its way into God's plans, things go sideways quickly. It is not natural, in our current culture, to receive. We earn everything. Nothing could be more detrimental to identity than believing you can earn holiness.

Something begins to change in our works when we understand that we are holy simply because God calls us holy. The following are two statements that are stating, theologically, the same thing. However, notice how differently you perceive these statements from each other.

1. You are called to live in holiness.

2. You are called holy.

As I said, these are theologically saying the same thing. Because you can only live in holiness if you are identified as holy, living in holiness is a matter of being called holy. If you are convinced that you are holy because God called you so, you will begin to naturally produce what you used to strive and fail at producing in religion: holiness.

What do I mean by being *convinced* you are holy?

When you get married, you have a ceremony, food, and dancing. It is a beautiful occasion, but something happens that day that shifts the entire rest of your life: you are joined in a covenant with another. This joining is made even more apparent by the wife changing her name to her husband's name. Do you have to be reminded to live like a married person continually?

No. You are convinced that you are identified as married based on the agreement to join in covenant with another. That marriage makes you a bride or groom to a groom or bride.

We are in covenant with God. However, we continually have to be reminded of that fact. The need to continually be assured of your covenant is a sign that there never was a fully-realized covenant. I do not, again, say that to question anyone's salvation but to allow you to think through how complete your salvation is. Did it introduce you to a religion of behavior modification, or did it convince you of a new identity? Your married identity has nothing to do with what you do but everything to do with whom you became at the time you said, "I do." Likewise, how you earn identity has nothing to do with works but whom you become when you say, "I do."

If you fully believe that you are who, as a son or daughter of God, you are, you will never again feel the weight of earning your holy identity by works. You will begin to live in holiness because you are holy. I know some will only read half of this chapter and say I am pushing a "do whatever you want" gospel. No, I am raising the standard for you to be more than what your behavioral mask says you are and, instead, calling for you to be authentically holy. Our conversation here is not about what you should be doing but about rewiring your idea of holiness to be orthodox so you can start to steward what God has given you in his generosity properly.

The second part of this root system is the blessing of a gauge that is built into our lives to constantly send us deeper into the Presence of God, where we belong. That gauge is what we do. I know, I just spent a whole section of this chapter talking about shifting our perspective from what we do to whom we become but now that we have put on the right pair of lenses to see things clearly, let us talk about works. What I am about to say is dangerous if you do not fully grasp the first section of this chapter. Our anchoring topic as we walk through holiness is identity. Remember that.

When we begin to act or live in ways that contradict who we are, it is a sign that there are some fractures in our covenant with the Lord. By fractures, I do not mean covenant is broken or destroyed; I mean some of the covenant fabric has not been consistently cared for. When we stop going deeper, get complacent, let life get too busy for the secret place intimate meet-up, stop tithing, grow apathetic toward the church, start expecting things out of relationships that those relationships cannot (and should not) give us, it is not a sign that we are losing our *holiness*, it is a sign that we are not living as what we are: *holy*.

Here, we do not respond with behavior-modified holiness because we have had our thinking changed to focus on identity. We instead see that due to a lack of presence with our covenant partner, we have started agreeing with a lie about who we are. To reiterate, actions cannot produce identity, but identity will always produce actions. Our aim is not what we do; our aim is always whom we are becoming that produces what we do. You could take a Tylenol for a headache when you have not had water all day, or you could drink water and fix the root cause of the headache. One is covering up what is still there (the issue), one is fixing what caused the symptom (the issue).

Symptoms of sickness are not a curse; they are a blessing. They are our body telling us something within is wrong that otherwise, we would never know about until it was too late. You know to get tested for the flu because you get achy and stuffy. If you had no symptoms whatsoever, you might be dying of something you had no idea you even had. We are always trying to get rid of symptoms because it is easy. Take a pill and they will go away. We never want to go through the process of discovering what caused the symptoms. Your body is working healthy when it shows you symptoms of things that can potentially change its overall health.

When we live in disagreement with who we are and realize it, it is not a sign that we are broken but a sign that we are healthy (with the caveat that we need to address what we see so that it does not eventually change the health of who we are). Conviction is healthy. *John 15* teaches that pruning is a blessing for bearing fruit. Conviction and condemnation, though, are two different things.

Conviction is when you realize you have done something that is not like you (disagrees with your identity) that needs to be addressed *at the root*. Condemnation is when you are criticized and disapproved of. I fear that the modern Church has replaced conviction for condemnation and, because of that, avoided true conviction altogether. Conviction is a sign of health. I want to feel convicted when my actions do not look like my identity because it is an invitation to go deeper into his Presence. Furthermore, the more I am convinced of who I am, the more my actions will align with who I am.

Romans 8:1, "There is now no condemnation for

those who are in Christ Jesus.".

2 Corinthians 7:8-11, "8 Even if I caused you sorrow by my letter, I do not regret it. Though I did regret it – I see that my letter hurt you, but only for a little while – 9 yet now I am happy, not because you were made sorry, but because your sorrow led you to repentance. For you became sorrowful as God intended and so were not harmed in any way by us. 10 Godly sorrow [conviction] *brings repentance that leads to salvation and leaves no regret, but worldly sorrow brings death. 11 See what this godly sorrow has produced in you: what earnestness, what eagerness to clear yourselves, what indignation, what alarm, what longing, what concern, what readiness to see justice done. At every point, you have proved yourselves to be innocent in this matter."*

Condemnation leads to rejection. In Christ, that is no longer a fear. You have been accepted not by works but by faith and receiving. Therefore, what you did not earn through works you cannot lose by works. Conviction leads to you living in the fullness of your acceptance. We need conviction. It is an unhealthy sign when there is no conviction in the body of Christ.

Proverbs 29:18, " Where there is no revelation, people cast off restraint; but blessed is the one who heeds wisdom's instruction."

Conviction toward our works is a significant piece of the prophetic vision we need to make sure we do not wander astray from (another translation of *cast off restrain*) who we are.

Holiness, in its proper context, is how we steward the generosity of God. The nature of God as a giver is something few have understood. It does not make sense to us that the God of creation longs to continually give to those who seem to be masters at screwing things up. However, I believe he is willing to trust us, even in the messiness of who we are, and wait for a generation who will understand how to steward the realization that God is a giver. We are that generation. We are the new holiness movement because we will be the generation to set a precedent for future generations as to what holy identity means. Therefore, we will reproduce holiness rather than living in holiness that is simply a set of good actions.

CHAPTER 14

WHAT GOD WANTS TO TAKE

———— ◆ ·◆· ◆ ————

Shel Silverstein wrote and illustrated a picture book called *"The Giving Tree,"* published in 1964. In it, he tells the story of a tree that wants nothing more in life than to give a boy what his heart desires. The boy's joy was the tree's joy, even if it meant the tree lost something for the boy to gain that joy. At the end of the book, the tree is left with only a stump, due to it giving everything else it had to the boy to make him happy. The tree then tells the now old man:

> *"I wish that I could give you something. . . but I have nothing left. I am just an old stump. I am sorry..."*

> *"I don't need very much now," said the boy, "just a quiet place to sit and rest. I am very tired."*

"Well," said the tree, straightening herself up as much as she could. "an old stump is good for sitting and resting. Come, Boy, sit down... and rest."

And the tree was happy...

This simple story has had a profound impact on me. This story was what launched me into the exploration that became this book. That God is the tree, if you will, that finds happiness in our happiness. Not just passive happiness, happiness that comes from receiving from the hand of our Creator. Happiness that comes through faith, trust, and permission.

Galatians 2:20, " I am crucified with Christ, and I no longer live, but Christ lives in me. The life I now live in the body, I live by faith in the Son of God, who loved me and gave himself for me."

We bear the likeness of God. Christ came as us so we could live as him. That is the simple gospel. What does it mean to bear the likeness of God? Sure, it means we love others, feed the hungry, and help the poor, but on a deeper level, what is it that makes us, "in the likeness of God?"

Could it be that we are most authentically *like God* when we share in his generosity? When I use the word *generosity*, I do not want you to hear tithing, though it sometimes includes tithing. I want you to hear the generosity that means a readiness to give more of something than necessary.

God showed his unfathomable love by giving himself, in the Messiah, to die as us (*Romans 5:8*). How do we return that to God? By giving up ourselves to live as him, or I would say, as we should have always been, not by dying on a cross, of course, but by trading our lives governed by the world around us for his life governed by the world within us.

I want to, for a moment, mention two ontological (the study of existence) viewpoints for us to fully grasp what Jesus has done for us and how we are to respond, with the help of some observances made by John H. Walton in his book, "*The Lost World of Genesis One*." There is the idea that something exists when it materializes and the idea that something exists when given its function.

For example, if I took a pile of legos and determined I would build a tower out of them, that tower would exist when it materialized in the finished product of my lego construction. It finds existence when it becomes a materialized product. When we filed the paperwork to become a 501c3 nonprofit organization church, we were officially a church in the government's eyes, but just because we materialized did not mean we existed. We were still six months away from a service, a message preached, or a song played. Anyone would say our church existed when we started having services and being, well, a church. In our church's example, it existed when it was given its intended function.

This ontological understanding is critical as it relates to how we see God, heaven, earth, and ultimately humanity. Most people believe the distance between heaven and earth is material. In other words, the earth is an evil substance, usually referred to as the flesh or the natural (both of which are used highly out of biblical context), and heaven is a floaty, ghostly, "other than" material usually called the spirit (also used highly out of biblical context).

The most popular scripture using this talk of flesh and spirit is in *Romans 8:5*, which says,

> *Those who live according to the flesh have their minds set on what the flesh desires, but those who live in accordance with the Spirit have their minds set on what the Spirit desires.*

Here, flesh refers, in the Greek, to that which is operating without the leading of the Spirit of God.

Not literal skin or the natural, physical, material world but those functionally operating incorrectly. Likewise, Spirit does not refer to a ghost trapped in your body (usually referred to wrongly as flesh) but that which illuminates your flesh in function. This verse is not talking about a material existence or living; it is talking about a functional existence or living. Why does this matter? Because if we only think in terms of material existence, when we marry the fact that God has redemption on his mind for the creation as a whole yet is giving us a new creation, the ideas will never work together, even though they are working together throughout scripture. However, if you see these two ideas in terms of functional existence, they work perfectly together because God plans to take the cosmos' material and give it its original (new) function.

This reasoning radically restores how we view everything in life and theology. God's space and our space are not separated by material but by function. If material separates them, the only way to encounter God's space is to die and go somewhere else. If function separates them, we can experience it in its fullness now by simple submission to having our function or purpose transformed.

While we are at it, let me remind you of what we

discussed in the chapter about the end. The Greek word used for the "new" creation talks about taking creation (including you and me) back to originality, not throwing everything away and starting over. See that in the lens of the conversation on function. The plan all along was not to keep going forward until we find redemption but to let the cross and Christ himself take us back to how we should have always been. Jesus came to give you a new, original, identity.

Now that we have gone down a few side trails let us come back to the topic of what we can give God. The greatest thing you can give God is who you thought you were before Jesus redeemed your story. That is what God wants and needs from us. He does not want your striving; he wants you to give him whom you used to be. Again, not in material but in function. The only way you can receive from God is to continually give him the pieces of the old you so that you are not holding them anymore.

God cannot make new (original) that which still functions as old (fake). God's image is the only image in creation. If you are not bearing God's image, you are not bearing an image at all. Whatever image you think you have is fake unless it is God's. If God is identified as a giver, we should be identified as givers because of our continual giving to him. Giving him what? What does not belong in us and what Jesus died for: who we were before we were refunctioned.

I differ from a lot of scholars in the West (not calling myself a scholar). I do not believe we are born into sin. I believe we are born into Christ but make the conscious decision to live in the delusion that we are separated from Christ, in our sin (or fall). At that point of misplacement, salvation comes to rip from us the sin delusion we have bought into once and for all and realigns us with who we truly are and always were (*see Luke 15 - None of the "lost" ever change owners. They are simply misplaced until they are found*). I also would define existence differently than many scholars today. I believe we existed before we materialized in that we were given our function before the foundation of the world. Prove it? *Ephesians 1:4 says, "For he chose us in him before the creation of the world to be holy and blameless in his sight. In love."*

The *us* in that verse is where many debates have heated up over the centuries. Of course, Paul is talking about humanity. The question is, are these believers who have been hand-picked by God and given a robotic path that has been prechosen for them to follow, as the Calvinists wrongly believe, or are these human beings as a whole who God predestined to be in Christ? I hold the latter belief. I believe every human being is born with a destiny to be the image-bearers they naturally are and that Abba will seek until he finds every one of his kids.

Some wrongfully see this as the type of thinking that Oprah and other modern influencers have made popular: that all roads lead to heaven. First, heaven is not the final and ultimate goal. New creation and resurrection is the final and ultimate goal. Second, Jesus is, to be clear, the only way (or road) to the Father. However, the New Testament makes it very clear that Jesus dealt Adam's fall a death blow (see *Romans 5* and *Colossians 1*). There is no more fall, if the incarnation, cross, resurrection, and ascension are legitimate realities (which they are). Every human being finds their existence in the finished work of Christ.

Your design is to be holy and blameless in his sight. For the son or daughter of God, you are holy and blameless in his sight not because of what you do, but because of your willingness to trade what you do for what he did (see chapter on stewarding generosity). Therefore we worship in the most excellent way when we most authentically become who we are in Christ: image and likeness bearers of God. We most authentically become who we are in Christ when we most authentically lose (or die to) any image or likeness absent of God. Something authentically dead means it cannot live again. It is dead and gone.

While this may sound like an easy thing to give God, and I believe it should be an easy thing to give him, it seems to be the most challenging thing you or I could ever do. God gives us the riches of everything he has, yet we struggle to give him the poverty of everything we have that does nothing but enslave us. We hold tightly, in our grip of comfort, deficient identity, weak expressions of honor, half-hearted devotion, and religious duties. The moment God, in love, begins to ask us for what we have in our hands, we start kicking and screaming, explaining to him why these are things we should be holding. We are known for our impoverished identity rather than our genuine identity. No one knows the real us because we are too busy holding tight to the fake us. We will not let anyone see behind the mask.

Creation is waiting for our unveiling. Behind a veil of broken identity, who we are is opaque, at best. Sometimes, glimpses of who is behind the veil sneak out, only to retract in another moment of hiding in the comfortable. Give the veil to God. Stop living as what you are not. Stop giving God the put-together you; it is not even very put together. Instead, give God the real you. The you who struggles with sin, struggles with identity, struggles with trust, and struggles with fitting in and let God show you that he nailed those pieces of you to a tree, through a man named Jesus Christ, so that you could walk out of a tomb with the same man, now free from all the things that he carried two days prior. If you died with Christ, you also were raised with Christ. It is not the raising with Christ we struggle with; it is the dying with Christ. The problem is, you cannot raise until you have died.

I am not, of course, talking about literally dying. I am talking about offering up whom you used to be as a living sacrifice so that God can resurrect you into your original function. Function gives existence to material, in the case of every living being. God is not as concerned with the material as he is the functional because a redeemed function can birth a redeemed material. In essence, you are laying down how you functioned and what your purpose was before Jesus so that you can inherit a new function, which is the one Jesus has.

We struggle so much with giving God what he desires (who we were) because it requires us to look very different from the culture around us (which should not be a surprise) and because it causes us to have to give our past a death blow. God deals with our past very differently than our culture deals with our past. For our culture, our past is our story. What has happened to us is who we should be, good or bad. For God, who we were and what has happened to us is only a part of our story so that we can understand how much reform has taken place within us. In Christ, we are called to, as *Isaiah 43:18* says, *forget the former things and not dwell on the past.* While everyone else in our culture is chained to their past like a pet weight they cannot let go of, we live free indeed where the only past that matters is the one where we existed in Christ before we took one breath.

You and I did not originate in our mother's womb. We originated in God. We just became manifested in the creation by way of our mother's womb. Your roots go way further back than your mother. God set you in motion long before the foundations of the earth. You are crucial to God's story. You are essential to creation's restoration. You are worth so much to him that he was willing to die on your behalf. We trample on God's design when we do not give him what he paid for: who we were apart from Jesus.

Give him the pieces of your old self as a worship offering and see if he will not throw open the floodgates of generosity on a son or daughter who finally looks like a son or daughter. You may even begin to notice creation responding to the fullness of your freedom.

This is the generosity of God, and everyone is included in it.

Made in the USA
Columbia, SC
25 July 2021